The authentic taste of Spain

tapas

The authentic taste of Spain

tapas

Parragon

Bath · New York · Singapore · Hong Kong · Cologne · Delhi · Melbourne

This is a Parragon Book
First published in 2009

Parragon
Queen Street House
4 Queen Street
Bath BA1 1HE, UK

ISBN 978-1-4075-6841-6

Printed in China

Cover and internal design by Talking Design
Introduction by Linda Doeser

Notes for the Reader

This book uses both metric and imperial measurements. Follow the same units of measurement throughout; do not mix metric and imperial. All spoon measurements are level: teaspoons are assumed to be 5 ml, and tablespoons are assumed to be 15 ml. Unless otherwise stated, milk is assumed to be full fat, eggs and individual vegetables are medium, and pepper is freshly ground black pepper.

The times given are an approximate guide only. Preparation times differ according to the techniques used by different people and the cooking times may also vary from those given. Optional ingredients, variations or serving suggestions have not been included in the calculations.

Recipes using raw or very lightly cooked eggs should be avoided by infants, the elderly, pregnant women, convalescents and anyone suffering from an illness. Pregnant and breastfeeding women are advised to avoid eating peanuts and peanut products. Sufferers from nut allergies should be aware that some of the ready-made ingredients used in the recipes in this book may contain nuts. Always check the packaging before use.

Always wear plastic gloves while working with chillies to protect your hands from the heat. A plastic bag placed over the hand that handles the chilli makes a simple makeshift glove. If you forget to cover your hands, make sure to wash them thoroughly afterward and, above all, resist any temptation to rub your eyes.

contents

INTRODUCTION

Nowadays there are tapas bars in cities across the world, yet not long ago hardly anyone outside Spain knew what tapas were. These delicious cocktail snacks range from tiny stuffed tomatoes to spicy prawn kebabs, from fat squares of warm tortilla to elegant seafood tartlets, and from simple cubes of serrano ham to fried baby eels served so hot that they burn your mouth.

Tapas have come a long way from their beginnings – in style as well as geographically. Spain has a hot and dry climate, so working hours and mealtimes were organised to make the most of the cooler parts of the day. Dinner was rarely eaten before late evening, so it became customary to drop into a bar on the way home from work for a glass of sherry, wine or cider. Bars in Andalucía, the region of southern Spain where sherry is produced, took to covering their customers' glasses with a slice of bread to keep flies out of the drinks. The word *tapa* means lid or cover. Later, they began to add a topping of ham or cheese, providing a complimentary snack.

From Andalucía, the custom of serving bar snacks spread across Spain, eventually giving rise to speciality tapas bars. Here customers order from an extensive menu and pay for these tasty little mouthfuls. The city of Barcelona in northern Spain is now arguably the tapas capital of the country.

Serving and eating tapas

Tapas have now become a course in their own right, rather like Italian antipasti and Greek "*meze*". A selection of dishes is often served as an hors d'oeuvre before the main course of a conventional meal. However, they have become so popular that people have taken to dining solely on tapas, choosing a larger selection to include a more extensive range of ingredients. Nevertheless, tapas haven't completely lost their historical beginnings and are still served as cocktail snacks in private houses.

Of course, home cooks can choose to serve tapas however they like. A table of tapas dishes is a popular choice for informal entertaining, because it tends to be colourful, fun and full of all sorts of different tastes and textures. Everyone is sure to find a favourite. Tapas dishes make great starters on more formal occasions and are a fuss-free way to overcome the difficulty of entertaining both vegetarian and meat-eating guests. Returning them to their roots, you may choose to serve them as tempting snacks with pre-dinner drinks and they also look fabulous on a buffet table at a party.

Some tapas are still served on the traditional base of bread or toast, which is often rubbed with garlic for extra flavour. Those with simple toppings, such as ham, cheese, mushrooms or prawns, are usually assembled in the kitchen and may be garnished with a herb sprig or twist of lemon. Toppings that more closely resemble a dip or pâté in texture are often served in a bowl with the toast served separately for guests to help themselves. This prevents the toast from becoming soggy. The tapas that come next in the evolutionary chain are those served in pastry shells, on mini-pizza bases or in little turnovers called empanadillas. Remember that all of these snacks should be bite-sized, so cut or stamp out the bases and shells accordingly.

Increasingly, tapas dishes have developed away from the idea of a bread or pastry base, although most are still finger

foods. These include olives, almonds, mussels served on the half shell, stuffed baby vegetables and eggs, and miniature kebabs. Some, such as deep-fried prawns and boiled new potatoes, are served with a dip. Finally, there are tapas that resemble small main dishes – meat, chicken, fish or vegetables cooked in a sauce. Once again, these should all be individual bite-sized morsels.

In Spain, tapas are almost always served in earthenware dishes. Hot foods can be cooked in them and cold snacks stay cool, but you don't have to go out and buy a whole new set of serving dishes. Use small dishes that suit the size of the serving. Dishes that are too big will make the contents look mean and inadequate, and if you are serving a selection of tapas, you'll probably run out of room on the table.

Provide a good supply of wooden cocktail sticks for spearing olives, prawns and so on. This helps limit the rather unhygienic practice of lots of different hands rummaging around in the serving dishes. If you're serving tapas as a starter or as an informal meal, you should also supply plates, knives and forks.

The authentic flavour of Spain

All the recipes in the following pages are based on both traditional and contemporary Spanish cooking and eating habits. Many of the ingredients will be familiar, even to those who have never visited the Mediterranean. Wherever a typically Spanish ingredient that may be difficult to obtain is specified, an alternative is suggested in the recipe or in the glossary of ingredients that follows.

ANCHOVIES: Fresh anchovies are easily spoiled so they are rarely available in inland cities in Spain, let alone in non-Mediterranean countries. Whole, salted anchovies, however, are widely used in tapas recipes and are well worth using if you can find them. Since they are not always available in supermarkets elsewhere, the recipes in this book suggest using canned anchovy fillets. Both types can be soaked in milk or water to remove some of the salt and whole anchovies should be filleted before use.

CHORIZO: This spicy, red sausage is also widely used in Mexican cooking. There are many varieties, some much hotter than others, but all contain pork and paprika, the spice producing the characteristic colour. It is important to distinguish between chorizo produced for slicing and eating and chorizo intended for cooking.

CLAMS: Small varieties, such as carpetshell, are the most popular for tapas dishes.

MANCHEGO: Made from sheep's milk, Manchego is Spain's best-known cheese. Originally produced in La Mancha, it is now made throughout the country and widely exported. It has a nutty flavour and is pale in colour. It is sold at all ages, from young fresco Manchego to mature cheese known as Iberico. Depending on the recipe, Parmesan or Gruyère cheese may be substituted.

OLIVE OIL: Spain is probably the world's largest producer of olive oil. It is characteristically deep-gold in colour and tends to be lighter and less pungent than Italian and

Greek oils.

OLIVES: Both green and black olives feature in many tapas dishes and a bowl of olives is a cocktail snack in its own right. Andalucía is the largest area of production and Gordal and Manzanilla olives are the best-known varieties. Green olives are frequently stuffed with pimientos, almonds or onion. In the Basque region, green olives stuffed with anchovies are a speciality.

PAPRIKA: This dark-red spice is made from ground red peppers. It may be mild, sometimes called sweet, or hot but is never so fiery as cayenne. In Spanish paprika production the peppers are smoked first, giving the spice a very distinctive flavour. Smoked paprika is available from some delicatessens and speciality shops.

PIMIENTOS: These are simply sweet peppers, but to non-Spaniards pimientos usually implies a variety of long, thin pepper that has been cooked, peeled and preserved in oil. They may be sliced or whole.

SAFFRON: Pungent with a slightly bitter taste, saffron is the world's most expensive spice. The neighbouring regions of La Mancha and Valencia are said to produce the best saffron in the world. There is no substitute.

SERRANO HAM: Jamón serrano simply means mountain ham and refers to ham that is salted for about a week and air-dried for six months. It is eaten raw, like Parma ham, which may be used as a substitute. Spanish ham is quite chewy in texture because it is carved along rather than against the grain.

SHERRY: This drink is a fortified wine. It gets its name from Jerez de la Frontera, the blisteringly hot, dry, chalky region of Andalucía where it is produced. Of course, tapas were developed to go with sherry in the first place but, in turn, sherry is often used to flavour tapas dishes. Other regions of Spain make a similar wine, notably Montilla from Montilla-Moriles and a sweet wine from Málaga.

VINEGAR: Both standard red and white wine vinegars are used in salad dressings and cooking, but Spain also produces speciality wine vinegars. Rioja vinegar, usually red, is full-bodied like the wine and mellow in flavour. Sherry vinegar is dark, mellow, rounded and smooth. Both are available from some delicatessens and speciality shops and sherry vinegar, in particular, is worth searching for if you want a truly authentic Spanish flavour to your food. However, balsamic vinegar may be used as a substitute.

Salads & Savoury Bites

SALAD OF MELON, CHORIZO & ARTICHOKES

SERVES 8
as part of a tapas meal

12 small globe artichokes

juice of $1/2$ lemon

2 tbsp Spanish olive oil

1 small orange-fleshed melon, such as cantaloupe

200 g/7 oz chorizo sausage, outer casing removed

a few sprigs of fresh tarragon or flat-leaf parsley, to garnish

DRESSING

3 tbsp Spanish extra-virgin olive oil

1 tbsp red wine vinegar

1 tsp prepared mustard

1 tbsp chopped fresh tarragon

salt and pepper

To prepare the artichokes, cut off the stalks. With your hands, break off the toughest outer leaves at the base until the tender inside leaves are visible. Using a pair of scissors, cut the spiky tips off the leaves. Using a sharp knife, pare the dark-green skin from the base and down the stem. As you prepare them, brush the cut surfaces of the artichokes with lemon juice to prevent discoloration. Alternatively, you could fill a bowl with cold water to which you have added a little lemon juice, and immerse the artichokes in the acidulated water to stop discoloration. Carefully remove the choke (the mass of silky hairs) by pulling it out with your fingers or by scooping it out with a spoon. It is very important to remove all the choke because the little barbs, if eaten, can irritate the throat. However, if you are using very young artichokes, you do not need to worry about removing the choke and you can include the stalk too, well scraped, because it will be quite tender. Cut the artichokes into quarters and brush them again with lemon juice.

Heat the olive oil in a large, heavy-based frying pan, then add the prepared artichokes and fry, stirring frequently, for 5 minutes, or until the artichoke leaves are golden brown. Remove from the pan, transfer to a large serving bowl and leave to cool.

To prepare the melon, cut in half and scoop out the seeds with a spoon. Cut the flesh into bite-sized cubes. Add to the cooled artichokes. Cut the chorizo into bite-sized chunks and add to the melon and artichokes.

To make the dressing, put all the ingredients in a small bowl and whisk together. Just before serving, pour the dressing over the prepared salad ingredients and toss together. Serve the salad garnished with tarragon or parsley sprigs.

OLIVES WRAPPED WITH ANCHOVIES

Using a sharp knife, halve each anchovy fillet lengthways.

Wrap a half-fillet around the middle of each olive, overlapping the ends, and secure with a wooden cocktail stick.

Repeat with another olive and anchovy fillet half and slide onto a cocktail stick.

Continue until all the ingredients are used. Serve immediately or cover until required.

MAKES 24

12 anchovy fillets in oil, drained

24 pimiento-stuffed green olives in oil, drained

SWEET ONION SALAD

Bring a large saucepan of lightly salted water to the boil. Add the onions and simmer for 20 minutes, or until tender. Drain and leave until cool enough to handle.

Thickly slice the onions and place in a shallow dish. Sprinkle over the parsley and olives and season to taste with pepper.

Whisk the vinegars and olive oil together in a bowl, then whisk in enough of the water to make a creamy vinaigrette.

Pour the dressing over the onions and serve at room temperature.

**SERVES 4–6
as part of a tapas
meal**

4 Spanish onions

2 tbsp chopped fresh
parsley

115 g/4 oz black olives,
stoned

1 tbsp sherry vinegar

2 tbsp red wine vinegar

125 ml/4 fl oz olive oil

about 1 tbsp water

salt and pepper

CRACKED MARINATED OLIVES

To allow the flavours of the marinade to penetrate the olives, place on a chopping board and, using a rolling pin, bash them lightly so that they crack slightly. Alternatively, use a sharp knife to cut a lengthways slit in each olive as far as the stone. Using the flat side of a broad knife, lightly crush each garlic clove. Using a pestle and mortar, crack the coriander seeds. Cut the lemon, with its rind, into small chunks.

Put the olives, garlic, coriander seeds, lemon chunks, thyme sprigs, fennel and chillies, if using, in a large bowl and toss together. Season with pepper to taste, but you should not need to add salt because preserved olives are usually salty enough. Pack the ingredients tightly into a glass jar with a lid. Pour in enough olive oil to cover the olives, then seal the jar tightly.

Leave the olives at room temperature for 24 hours, then marinate in the refrigerator for at least 1 week but preferably 2 weeks before serving. From time to time, gently give the jar a shake to re-mix the ingredients. Return the olives to room temperature and remove from the oil to serve. Provide cocktail sticks for spearing the olives. Serve with crusty bread.

**SERVES 8
as part of a tapas
meal**

450 g/1 lb can or jar
unstoned large green
olives, drained

4 garlic cloves, peeled

2 tsp coriander seeds

1 small lemon

4 sprigs of fresh thyme

4 feathery stalks of
fennel

2 small fresh red chillies
(optional)

pepper

Spanish extra-virgin

olive oil, to cover

crusty bread, to serve

SAUTÉED GARLIC MUSHROOMS

**SERVES 6
as part of a tapas
meal**

450 g/1 lb button
mushrooms

5 tbsp Spanish olive oil

2 garlic cloves, finely
chopped

squeeze of lemon juice

salt and pepper

4 tbsp chopped fresh
flat-leaf parsley, plus
extra sprigs to garnish

crusty bread, to serve

Wipe or brush clean the mushrooms, then trim off the stalks close to the caps. Cut any large mushrooms in half or into quarters. Heat the olive oil in a large, heavy-based frying pan, add the garlic and fry for 30–60 seconds, or until lightly browned. Add the mushrooms and sauté over a high heat, stirring most of the time, until the mushrooms have absorbed all the oil in the pan.

Reduce the heat to low. When the juices have come out of the mushrooms, increase the heat again and sauté for 4–5 minutes, stirring most of the time, until the juices have almost evaporated. Add a squeeze of lemon juice and season to taste with salt and pepper. Stir in the parsley and cook for a further minute.

Transfer the sautéed mushrooms to a warmed serving dish, garnish with parsley sprigs and serve piping hot or warm. Accompany with chunks or slices of crusty bread for mopping up the garlic cooking juices.

RUSSIAN SALAD

Put the eggs in a saucepan, cover with cold water and slowly bring to the boil. Immediately reduce the heat to very low, cover and simmer gently for 10 minutes. As soon as the eggs are cooked, drain them and put under cold running water until they are cold. By doing this quickly, you will prevent a black ring from forming around the egg yolk. Gently tap the eggs to crack the egg shells and leave them until cold.

Meanwhile, put the potatoes in a large saucepan of cold, salted water and bring to the boil. Reduce the heat and simmer for 7 minutes, or until just tender. Add the beans and peas to the saucepan for the last 2 minutes of cooking. Drain well, splash under cold running water, then leave the vegetables to cool completely.

Cut the carrots into julienne strips about 2.5 cm/1 inch in length. Flake the tuna into large chunks. When the potatoes, beans and peas are cold, put them in a large bowl. Add the carrot strips and the flaked tuna and very gently toss the ingredients together. Transfer the vegetables and tuna to a salad bowl or large serving dish.

In a jug, stir the lemon juice into the mayonnaise to thin it slightly, then stir in the garlic and season to taste with salt and pepper. Drizzle the mayonnaise dressing over the vegetables and tuna.

Scatter the gherkins, olives and capers into the salad and finally sprinkle over the parsley and dill. You can store the salad in the refrigerator but return to room temperature before serving. Just before serving, crack the shells of the eggs all over and remove them. Slice the eggs into wedges, add them to the salad and garnish with dill sprigs.

**SERVES 8
as part of a tapas
meal**

2 eggs

450 g/1 lb baby new
potatoes, quartered

115 g/4 oz green
beans, cut into 2.5-cm/
1-inch lengths

115 g/4 oz frozen peas

115 g/4 oz carrots

200 g/7 oz canned
tuna steak in olive oil,
drained

2 tbsp lemon juice

8 tbsp mayonnaise

1 garlic clove, crushed

salt and pepper

4 small gherkins, sliced

8 stoned black olives,
halved

1 tbsp capers

1 tbsp chopped fresh
flat-leaf parsley

1 tbsp chopped fresh
dill, plus extra sprigs to
garnish

SALTED ALMONDS

**SERVES 6–8
as part of a tapas
meal**

225 g/8 oz whole
almonds, in their skins
or blanched
(see method)

4 tbsp Spanish olive oil

coarse sea salt

1 tsp paprika or ground
cumin (optional)

Preheat the oven to 180°C/350°F/Gas Mark 4. Fresh almonds in their skins are superior in taste, but blanched almonds are much more convenient. If the almonds are not blanched, put them in a bowl, cover with boiling water for 3–4 minutes, then plunge them into cold water for 1 minute. Drain them well in a sieve, then slide off the skins between your fingers. Dry the almonds well on kitchen paper.

Put the olive oil in a roasting tin and swirl it around so that it covers the base. Add the almonds and toss them in the tin so that they are evenly coated in the oil, then spread them out in a single layer.

Roast the almonds in the oven for 20 minutes, or until they are light golden brown, tossing several times during the cooking. Drain the almonds on kitchen paper, then transfer them to a bowl.

While the almonds are still warm, sprinkle with plenty of sea salt, and the paprika or cumin if using, and toss well together to coat. Serve the almonds warm or cold. The almonds are at their best when served freshly cooked so, if possible, cook them on the day that you plan to eat them. However, they can be stored in an airtight container for up to 3 days.

TOMATO & OLIVE SALAD

First, make the dressing. Whisk the vinegar, olive oil, garlic and paprika together in a bowl. Season to taste with salt and reserve.

Place the tomatoes, olives, cucumber, shallots and capers in a separate bowl. Pour over the dressing and toss lightly.

Line 6 individual serving bowls with chicory leaves. Spoon an equal quantity of the salad into the centre of each and serve.

**SERVES 6
as part of a tapas
meal**

2 tbsp sherry vinegar
or red wine vinegar

5 tbsp Spanish olive oil

1 garlic clove, finely
chopped

1 tsp paprika

salt

4 tomatoes, peeled and
diced

12 anchovy-stuffed or
pimiento-stuffed olives

$1/2$ cucumber, peeled
and diced

2 shallots,
finely chopped

1 tbsp pickled capers
in brine, drained

2–3 heads of chicory,
separated into leaves

TUNA, EGG & POTATO SALAD

**SERVES 4
as part of a tapas
meal**

350 g/12 oz new
potatoes, unpeeled

1 hard-boiled egg,
cooled and shelled

3 tbsp olive oil

1¹/₂ tbsp white wine
vinegar

salt and pepper

115 g/4 oz canned
tuna in oil, drained and
flaked

2 shallots,
finely chopped

1 tomato,
peeled and diced

2 tbsp chopped fresh
parsley

Cook the potatoes in a saucepan of lightly salted boiling water for 10 minutes, then remove from the heat, cover and leave to stand for 15–20 minutes, or until tender.

Meanwhile, slice the egg, then cut each slice in half. Whisk the olive oil and vinegar together in a bowl and season to taste with salt and pepper. Spoon a little of the vinaigrette into a serving dish to coat the base.

Drain the potatoes, peel and thinly slice. Place half the slices over the base of the dish, season to taste with salt, then top with half the tuna, half the egg slices and half the shallots. Pour over half the remaining dressing. Make a second layer with the remaining potato slices, tuna, egg and shallots, then pour over the remaining dressing.

Finally, top the salad with the tomato and parsley, cover with clingfilm and leave to stand in a cool place for 1–2 hours before serving.

CHORIZO IN RED WINE

Before you begin, bear in mind that this dish is best if prepared the day before you are planning to serve it.

Using a fork, prick the chorizo sausage in 3 or 4 places. Put it in a large saucepan and pour in the wine. Bring the wine to the boil, then reduce the heat, cover and simmer gently for 15–20 minutes. Transfer the chorizo and wine to a bowl or dish, cover, and leave the sausage to marinate in the wine for 8 hours or overnight.

The next day, remove the chorizo from the bowl or dish and reserve the wine for later. Remove the outer casing from the chorizo and cut the sausage into 5-mm/¼-inch slices.

Place the slices in a large, heavy-based frying pan or flameproof serving dish.

If you are adding the brandy, pour it into a small saucepan and heat gently. Pour the brandy over the chorizo slices, stand well back and set alight. When the flames have died down, shake the pan gently, add the reserved wine to the pan and cook over a high heat until almost all of the wine has evaporated.

Serve the chorizo in red wine piping hot, in the dish in which it was cooked, sprinkled with parsley to garnish. Accompany with chunks or slices of bread to mop up the juices and provide cocktail sticks to spear the pieces of chorizo.

**SERVES 6
as part of a tapas
meal**

200 g/7 oz chorizo
sausage

200 ml/7 fl oz Spanish
red wine

2 tbsp brandy
(optional)

chopped fresh flat-leaf
parsley, to garnish

crusty bread, to serve

TUNA ROLLS

Preheat the grill to high. Place the peppers on a baking sheet and cook under the preheated grill, turning frequently, for 10 minutes, or until the skin is blackened and blistered all over. Using tongs, transfer to a polythene bag, tie the top and leave to cool.

Meanwhile, whisk the olive oil, lemon juice, vinegar, garlic, paprika, chilli flakes and sugar together in a small bowl.

When the peppers are cool enough to handle, peel off the skins, then cut the flesh into quarters lengthways and deseed. Place the pepper pieces in a non-metallic dish and pour over the dressing, turning to coat. Leave to stand in a cool place for 30 minutes.

Rub the salt off the capers and mix with the tuna. Drain the pepper pieces, reserving the dressing. Divide the tuna mixture between the pepper pieces and roll up. Secure with a wooden cocktail stick. Place the tuna rolls on a serving platter, spoon over the dressing and serve at room temperature.

SERVES 4
as part of a tapas
meal

3 red peppers

125 ml/4 fl oz olive oil

2 tbsp lemon juice

5 tbsp red wine vinegar

2 garlic cloves,
finely chopped

1 tsp paprika

1 tsp dried chilli flakes

2 tsp sugar

2 tbsp salted capers

200 g/7 oz canned
tuna in oil, drained and
flaked

GREEN BEANS WITH PINE KERNELS

Heat the oil in a large, heavy-based frying pan, add the pine kernels and fry for about 1 minute, stirring all the time and shaking the pan, until light golden brown. Using a slotted spoon, remove the pine kernels from the pan, drain well on kitchen paper, then transfer to a bowl. Reserve the oil in the frying pan for later. Add the paprika, according to taste, to the pine kernels, stir together until coated, and then set aside.

Top and tail the green beans and remove any strings if necessary. Put the beans in a saucepan, pour over boiling water, return to the boil and cook for 5 minutes, or until tender but still firm. Drain well in a colander.

Reheat the oil in the frying pan, add the onion and fry for 5–10 minutes, or until softened and beginning to brown. Add the garlic and fry for a further 30 seconds.

Add the beans to the pan and cook for 2–3 minutes, tossing together with the onion until heated through. Season the beans to taste with salt and pepper.

Turn the contents of the pan into a warmed serving dish, sprinkle over the lemon juice and toss together. Scatter over the golden pine kernels and serve hot.

SERVES 8
as part of a tapas meal

2 tbsp Spanish olive oil

50 g/1³/₄ oz pine kernels

¹/₂–1 tsp paprika

450 g/1 lb green beans

1 small onion, finely chopped

1 garlic clove, finely chopped

salt and pepper

juice of ¹/₂ lemon

STUFFED PIMIENTOS

**MAKES 7–8
as part of a tapas
meal**

185 g/6¹/₂ oz canned
or bottled whole
pimientos del piquillo
(chargrilled sweet red
peppers)

fresh herb sprigs,
to garnish

**COTTAGE CHEESE
AND HERB FILLING**

225 g/8 oz cottage
cheese

1 tsp lemon juice

1 garlic clove, crushed

4 tbsp chopped fresh
flat-leaf parsley

1 tbsp chopped fresh
mint

1 tbsp chopped fresh
oregano

salt and pepper

OR

**TUNA MAYONNAISE
FILLING**

200 g/7 oz canned
tuna steak in olive oil,
drained

5 tbsp mayonnaise

2 tsp lemon juice

2 tbsp chopped fresh
flat-leaf parsley

salt and pepper

OR

**GOAT'S CHEESE AND
OLIVE FILLING**

50 g/1³/₄ oz stoned
black olives,
finely chopped

200 g/7 oz soft goat's
cheese

1 garlic clove, crushed

salt and pepper

There is actually a choice of fillings provided in this recipe – the final decision is yours. Lift the peppers from the jar, reserving the oil for later.

To make the cottage cheese and herb filling, put the cottage cheese in a bowl and add the lemon juice, garlic, parsley, mint and oregano. Mix well together. Season to taste with salt and pepper.

To make the tuna and mayonnaise filling, put the tuna in a bowl and add the mayonnaise, lemon juice and parsley. Add 1 tablespoon of the reserved oil from the jar of pimientos and mix well. Season to taste with salt and pepper.

To make the goat's cheese and olive filling, put the olives in a bowl and add the goat's cheese, garlic and 1 tablespoon of the reserved oil from the jar of pimientos. Mix well together. Season to taste with salt and pepper.

Using a teaspoon, heap the filling of your choice into each pimiento. Put in the refrigerator and chill for at least 2 hours until firm.

To serve the pimientos, arrange them on a serving plate and, if necessary, wipe with kitchen paper to remove any of the filling that has spread over the skins. Garnish with fresh herb sprigs.

ARTICHOKE HEARTS & ASPARAGUS

Trim and discard the coarse, woody ends of the asparagus spears. Make sure all the stems are about the same length, then tie them together loosely with clean kitchen string. If you have an asparagus steamer, you don't need to tie the stems together – just place them in the basket.

Bring a tall saucepan of lightly salted water to the boil. Add the asparagus, making sure that the tips are protruding above the water, reduce the heat and leave to simmer for 10–15 minutes, or until tender. Test by piercing a stem just above the water level with the point of a sharp knife. Drain, refresh under cold running water and drain again.

Cut the asparagus spears into 2.5-cm/1-inch pieces, keeping the tips intact. Cut the artichoke hearts into small wedges and combine with the asparagus in a bowl.

Whisk the orange juice, orange rind, walnut oil and mustard together in a bowl and season to taste with salt and pepper. If serving immediately, pour the dressing over the artichoke hearts and asparagus and toss lightly.

Arrange the salad leaves in individual serving dishes and top with the artichoke and asparagus mixture. Serve immediately. Alternatively, store the salad, covered, in the refrigerator and add the dressing just before serving.

**SERVES 4
as part of a tapas
meal**

**450 g/1 lb asparagus
spears**

**400 g/14 oz canned
artichoke hearts,
drained and rinsed**

**2 tbsp freshly
squeezed orange juice**

**$^{1}/_{2}$ tsp finely grated
orange rind**

2 tbsp walnut oil

1 tsp Dijon mustard

salt and pepper

salad leaves, to serve

MIXED BEANS

SEVES 4–6
as part of a tapas
meal

175 g/6 oz shelled
fresh or frozen broad
beans

115 g/4 oz fresh or
frozen French beans

115 g/4 oz mangetouts,
trimmed

1 shallot,
finely chopped

6 fresh mint sprigs

4 tbsp Spanish olive oil

1 tbsp sherry vinegar

1 garlic clove,
finely chopped

salt and pepper

Bring a large saucepan of lightly salted water to the boil. Add the broad beans, reduce the heat, cover and simmer for 7 minutes. Remove the beans with a slotted spoon, plunge into cold water and drain. Remove and discard the outer skins.

Meanwhile, return the saucepan of salted water to the boil. Add the French beans and return to the boil again. Drain and refresh under cold running water. Drain well.

Mix the broad beans, French beans, mangetouts and shallot together in a bowl. Strip the leaves from the mint sprigs, reserve half and add the remainder to the bean mixture. Finely chop the reserved mint.

Whisk the olive oil, vinegar, garlic and chopped mint together in a separate bowl and season to taste with salt and pepper. Pour the dressing over the bean mixture and toss lightly to coat. Cover with clingfilm and leave to chill until required.

ROASTED PEPPER SALAD

Preheat the grill. Place all the peppers on a wire rack or grill pan and cook under a hot grill for 10 minutes, or until their skins have blackened and blistered all over, turning them frequently.

Remove the roasted peppers from the heat, put them in a bowl and immediately cover tightly with a clean, damp tea towel.

Alternatively, you can put the peppers in a polythene bag. You will find that the steam helps to soften the skins and makes it easier to remove them. Leave the peppers for about 15 minutes until they are cool enough to handle.

Holding one pepper at a time over a clean bowl, use a sharp knife to make a small hole in the base and gently squeeze out the juices and reserve them. Still holding the pepper over the bowl, carefully peel off the blackened skin with your fingers or a knife and discard it. Cut the peppers in half and remove the stem, core and seeds, then cut each pepper into neat thin strips. Arrange the pepper strips attractively on a serving dish.

To the reserved pepper juices add the olive oil, sherry vinegar, garlic, sugar, and salt and pepper to taste. Whisk together until combined. Drizzle the dressing evenly over the salad.

Scatter the capers, olives and chopped marjoram over the salad, garnish with marjoram sprigs and serve at room temperature.

**SERVES 8
as part of a tapas
meal**

3 red peppers

3 yellow peppers

5 tbsp Spanish
extra-virgin olive oil

2 tbsp dry sherry
vinegar or lemon juice

2 garlic cloves, crushed

pinch of sugar

salt and pepper

1 tbsp capers

8 small black Spanish
olives, stoned

2 tbsp chopped fresh
marjoram, plus extra
sprigs to garnish

STUFFED PEPPERS

MAKES 6

6 tbsp olive oil, plus a
little extra for rubbing
on peppers

2 onions, finely chopped

2 garlic cloves, crushed

140 g/5 oz Spanish
short-grain rice

55 g/2 oz raisins

55 g/2 oz pine kernels

40 g/1¹/₂ oz fresh
parsley, finely chopped

1 tbsp tomato purée
dissolved in 700 ml/
1¹/₄ pints hot water

6 red, green or yellow
peppers
(or a mix of colours)

salt and pepper

Preheat the oven to 200°C/400°F/Gas Mark 6. Heat the oil in a shallow, heavy-based, flameproof casserole. Add the onions and fry for 3 minutes. Add the garlic and fry for a further 2 minutes, or until the onions are soft but not brown.

Stir in the rice, raisins and pine kernels until all are coated in the oil, then add half the parsley, and salt and pepper to taste. Stir in the tomato purée and bring to the boil. Reduce the heat and leave to simmer, uncovered, shaking the casserole frequently, for 20 minutes or until the rice is tender, the liquid is absorbed and small holes appear on the surface. Watch carefully because the raisins can catch and burn. Stir in the remaining parsley, then leave to cool slightly.

While the rice is simmering, cut the top off each pepper and reserve. Remove the core and seeds from each pepper.

Divide the stuffing equally between the peppers. Use wooden cocktail sticks to secure the tops back in place. Lightly rub each pepper with olive oil and arrange in a single layer in a baking dish. Bake in the preheated oven for 30 minutes, or until the peppers are tender. Serve hot or leave to cool to room temperature.

Egg & Cheese Dishes

STUFFED CHERRY TOMATOES

SERVES 8
as part of a tapas meal

24 cherry tomatoes

fresh dill sprigs, to garnish

ANCHOVY AND OLIVE FILLING

50 g/1¾ oz canned anchovy fillets in olive oil

8 pimiento-stuffed green olives, finely chopped

2 large hard-boiled eggs, finely chopped

pepper

OR

CRAB SALAD FILLING

175 g/6 oz canned crabmeat, drained

4 tbsp mayonnaise

1 tbsp chopped fresh flat-leaf parsley

salt and pepper

OR

BLACK OLIVE AND CAPER FILLING

12 stoned black olives

3 tbsp capers

6 tbsp Aïoli (see page 164)

salt and pepper

Several different choices of filling have been given in this recipe, so make a decision before you begin or, of course, you could make a selection of each. Simply cut the filling quantities to stuff the corresponding number of tomatoes. If necessary, cut and discard a very thin slice from the stalk end of each tomato to make the bases flat and stable.

Cut a thin slice from the smooth end of each tomato and discard. Using a serrated knife or teaspoon, loosen the pulp and seeds of each and scoop out, discarding the flesh. Turn the scooped-out tomatoes upside down on kitchen paper and leave to drain for 5 minutes.

To make the anchovy and olive filling, drain the anchovies, reserving the oil for later, chop finely and put in a bowl. Add the olives and hard-boiled eggs. Pour in a trickle of oil from the drained anchovies to moisten the mixture, season with pepper (don't add salt to season because the anchovies will provide enough) and mix well together.

To make the crab salad filling, put the crabmeat, mayonnaise and parsley in a bowl and mix well together. Season the filling to taste with salt and pepper.

To make the black olive and caper filling, put the olives and capers on kitchen paper to drain them well, then chop finely and put in a bowl. Add the Aïoli and mix well together. Season the filling to taste with salt and pepper.

Fill a piping bag fitted with a 2-cm/¾-inch plain nozzle with the filling of your choice and use to pack the filling into the hollow tomato shells. Store the tomatoes in the refrigerator, then serve with fresh dill sprigs.

FRIED MANCHEGO CHEESE

Slice the cheese into triangular shapes about 2 cm/³/₄ inch thick or alternatively into cubes measuring about the same size. Put the flour in a polythene bag and season with salt and pepper to taste. Break the egg into a shallow dish and beat together with the water. Spread the breadcrumbs onto a plate.

Toss the cheese pieces in the flour so that they are evenly coated, then dip the cheese in the egg mixture. Finally, dip the cheese in the breadcrumbs so that the pieces are coated on all sides. Transfer to a large plate and store in the refrigerator until you are ready to serve them.

Just before serving, heat about 2.5 cm/1 inch of the groundnut oil in a large, heavy-based frying pan or heat the oil in a deep fryer to 180–190°C/350–375°F, or until a cube of bread browns in 30 seconds. Add the cheese pieces, in batches of about 4 or 5 pieces so that the temperature of the oil does not drop, and fry for 1–2 minutes, turning once, until the cheese is just beginning to melt and they are golden brown on all sides. Do make sure that the oil is hot enough otherwise the coating on the cheese will take too long to become crisp and the cheese inside may ooze out.

Using a slotted spoon, remove the fried cheese from the frying pan or deep fryer and drain well on kitchen paper. Serve the fried cheese pieces hot, accompanied by cocktail sticks with which to spear them.

**SERVES 6–8
as part of a tapas
meal**

200 g/7 oz Manchego
cheese

3 tbsp plain flour

1 egg

1 tsp water

85 g/3 oz fresh white
or brown breadcrumbs

groundnut oil,
for deep-frying

salt and pepper

DEVILLED EGGS

MAKES 16

8 large eggs

2 whole pimientos
(sweet red peppers)
from a jar or can

8 green stoned olives,
retain 16 slices
for garnishing

5 tbsp mayonnaise

8 drops Tabasco sauce

large pinch of cayenne
pepper

salt and pepper

paprika, for dusting

sprigs of fresh dill,
to garnish

To cook the eggs, put them in a saucepan, cover with cold water and slowly bring to the boil. Immediately reduce the heat to very low, cover and simmer gently for 10 minutes. As soon as the eggs are cooked, drain them and put under cold running water until they are cold. By doing this quickly, it will prevent a black ring from forming around the egg yolk. Gently tap the eggs to crack the egg shells and leave them until cold. When cold, crack the shells all over and remove them.

Using a stainless steel knife, halve the eggs lengthways, then carefully remove the yolks. Put the yolks in a nylon sieve, set over a bowl, and rub through, then mash them with a wooden spoon or fork. If necessary, rinse the egg whites under cold water and dry very carefully.

Put the pimientos on kitchen paper to dry well, then chop them finely, reserving a few strips. Finely chop the olives. If you are going to pipe the filling into the eggs, you need to chop the pimientos and olives very finely so that they will go through a 1-cm/½-inch nozzle. Add the chopped pimientos and most of the chopped olives to the mashed egg yolks, reserving the pimiento slices to garnish. Add the mayonnaise, mix well together, then add the Tabasco sauce, cayenne pepper, and salt and pepper to taste.

For a grand finale, put the egg yolk mixture into a piping bag fitted with a 1-cm/½-inch plain nozzle and pipe the mixture into the hollow egg whites. Alternatively, for a simpler finish, use a teaspoon to spoon the prepared filling into each egg half.

Arrange the eggs on a serving plate. Add a small strip of the reserved pimientos and a piece of sliced olive to the top of each stuffed egg. Dust with a little paprika and garnish with dill sprigs.

CHORIZO & CHEESE TORTILLA

Cook the potatoes in a small saucepan of lightly salted boiling water for 15–20 minutes, or until just tender. Drain and leave until cool enough to handle, then dice.

Heat the olive oil in a large frying pan with a heatproof handle that can safely be placed under the grill. Add the onion, pepper and tomatoes and cook over a low heat, stirring occasionally, for 5 minutes. Add the diced potatoes and chorizo and cook for a further 5 minutes. Meanwhile, preheat the grill to high.

Beat the eggs with the water, and salt and pepper to taste, in a large bowl. Pour the mixture into the frying pan and cook for 8–10 minutes, or until the underside is set. Lift the edge of the tortilla occasionally to allow the uncooked egg to run underneath. Sprinkle the grated cheese over the tortilla and place under the hot grill for 3 minutes, or until the top is set and the cheese has melted. Serve, warm or cold, cut into thin wedges.

**SERVES 8
as part of a tapas
meal**

2 small potatoes
(peeled)

4 tbsp olive oil

1 small onion, chopped

1 red pepper,
deseeded and chopped

2 tomatoes, deseeded
and diced

140 g/5 oz chorizo
sausage, finely chopped

8 large eggs

2 tbsp cold water

55 g/2 oz mature
Mahón, Manchego or
Parmesan cheese,
grated

salt and pepper

BAKED TOMATO NESTS

MAKES 4

4 large ripe tomatoes

4 large eggs

4 tbsp double cream

4 tbsp grated mature
Mahón, Manchego or
Parmesan cheese

salt and pepper

Preheat the oven to 180°C/350°F/Gas Mark 4. Cut a slice off the top of each tomato and, using a teaspoon, carefully scoop out the pulp and seeds without piercing the shells. Turn the tomato shells upside down on kitchen paper and leave to drain for 15 minutes. Season the insides of the shells with salt and pepper.

Place the tomatoes in an ovenproof dish just large enough to hold them in a single layer. Carefully break one egg into each tomato shell, then top with one tablespoon of cream and one tablespoon of grated cheese.

Bake in the preheated oven for 15–20 minutes, or until the eggs are just set. Serve hot.

BROAD BEANS WITH CHEESE & PRAWNS

Bring a large saucepan of lightly salted water to the boil. Add the broad beans and one thyme sprig, then reduce the heat, cover and simmer for 7 minutes. Drain well, refresh under cold running water and drain again.

Unless the broad beans are very young, remove and discard the outer skins. Place the beans in a bowl and add the prawns and cheese.

Chop the remaining thyme sprig. Whisk the olive oil, lemon juice, garlic and chopped thyme together in a separate bowl and season to taste with salt and pepper.

Pour the dressing over the bean mixture, toss lightly and serve.

**SERVES 6
as part of a tapas
meal**

500 g/1 lb 2 oz shelled
fresh or frozen broad
beans

2 fresh thyme sprigs

225 g/8 oz cooked
peeled prawns

225 g/8 oz Queso
Majorero or Gruyère
cheese, diced

6 tbsp olive oil

2 tbsp lemon juice

1 garlic clove, finely
chopped

salt and pepper

ASPARAGUS & FRIED EGGS

**SERVES 6
as part of a tapas
meal**

500 g/1 lb 2 oz
asparagus spears

2 tbsp olive oil

6 eggs

Trim and discard the coarse, woody ends of the asparagus spears. Make sure all the stems are about the same length, then tie them together loosely with clean kitchen string. If you have an asparagus steamer, you don't need to tie the stems together – just place them in the basket.

Bring a tall saucepan of lightly salted water to the boil. Add the asparagus, making sure that the tips are protruding above the water, reduce the heat and leave to simmer for 10–15 minutes, or until tender. Test by piercing a stem just above the water level with the point of a sharp knife.

Meanwhile, heat a little of the olive oil in a large, heavy-based frying pan. Add two eggs, if there is enough room, and fry over a medium–low heat until the whites are just set and the yolks are still runny. Transfer to warmed serving plates and cook the remaining eggs in the same way.

Drain the asparagus and divide the spears between the plates. Serve immediately.

ROASTED PEPPERS WITH FIERY CHEESE

Preheat the grill to high. Place the peppers, skin-side up, in a single layer on a baking sheet. Cook under the hot grill for 8–10 minutes, or until the skins have blistered and blackened. Using tongs, transfer to a polythene bag, tie the top and leave to cool.

When the peppers are cool enough to handle, peel off the skin with your fingers or a knife and discard it. Place on a serving plate and sprinkle over the cheese.

Whisk the honey and vinegar together in a bowl and season to taste with salt and pepper. Pour the dressing over the peppers, cover and leave to chill until required.

**SERVES 6
as part of a tapas
meal**

1 red pepper, halved
and deseeded

1 orange pepper,
halved and deseeded

1 yellow pepper,
halved and deseeded

115 g/4 oz Afuega'l Pitu
cheese or other hot
spiced cheese, diced

1 tbsp clear honey

1 tbsp sherry vinegar

salt and pepper

MEDITERRANEAN SCRAMBLED EGGS

**SERVES 4–6
as part of a tapas
meal**

3–4 tbsp Spanish
olive oil

1 large onion,
finely chopped

1 large red pepper,
deseeded and chopped

1 large green pepper,
deseeded and chopped

2 large tomatoes,
peeled, deseeded and
chopped

55 g/2 oz chorizo
sausage, sliced thinly,
outer casing removed,
if preferred

35 g/1¹/₄ oz butter

10 large eggs, lightly
beaten

salt and pepper

4–6 thick slices
country-style bread,
toasted, to serve

Heat two tablespoons of olive oil in a large, heavy-based frying pan over a medium heat. Add the onion and peppers and cook for 5 minutes, or until the vegetables are softened but not browned. Add the tomatoes and heat through. Transfer to a heatproof plate and keep warm in a preheated low oven.

Add another tablespoon of oil to the frying pan. Add the chorizo and cook for 30 seconds, just to warm through and flavour the oil. Add the sausage to the reserved vegetables.

Add a little extra olive oil, if necessary, to bring it back to two tablespoons. Add the butter and allow to melt. Season the eggs with salt and pepper, then add to the pan and scramble until cooked to the desired degree of firmness. Return the vegetables to the pan and stir through. Serve immediately with hot toast.

HARD-BOILED EGGS WITH PEPPERS

Bring a saucepan of water to the boil. Add the peppers and blanch for 5 minutes. Drain, refresh under cold running water and drain well again. Pat dry with kitchen paper and cut into thin strips.

Arrange the slices of egg in serving dishes and sprinkle over the pepper strips.

Alternatively, make a lattice pattern with the pepper strips.

Whisk the vinegar, olive oil, shallot, dill and sugar together in a bowl and season to taste with salt and pepper. Spoon the dressing over the eggs and serve immediately.

**SERVES 6
as part of a tapas
meal**

2 red peppers,
halved and deseeded

6 hard-boiled eggs,
cooled, shelled and
sliced

2 tbsp white wine
vinegar

5 tbsp olive oil

1 shallot, finely chopped

2 tsp chopped fresh dill

pinch of sugar

salt and pepper

EGGS & CHEESE

Cut the eggs in half lengthways and, using a teaspoon, carefully scoop out the yolks into a fine sieve, reserving the egg white halves. Rub the yolks through the sieve into a bowl and add the grated cheese, mayonnaise, chives, chilli, and salt and pepper to taste.

Spoon the filling into the egg white halves.

Arrange a bed of lettuce on individual serving plates and top with the eggs. Cover and leave to chill until ready to serve.

SERVES 6
as part of a tapas
meal

6 hard-boiled eggs, cooled and shelled

3 tbsp grated Manchego or Cheddar cheese

1–2 tbsp mayonnaise

2 tbsp snipped fresh chives

1 fresh red chilli, deseeded and finely chopped

salt and pepper

lettuce leaves, to serve

SPINACH & MUSHROOM TORTILLA

Heat the olive oil in a frying pan with a heatproof handle that can safely be placed under the grill. Add the shallots and cook over a low heat, stirring occasionally, for 5 minutes, or until softened. Add the mushrooms and cook, stirring frequently, for a further 4 minutes. Add the spinach, increase the heat to medium and cook, stirring frequently, for 3–4 minutes, or until wilted. Reduce the heat, season to taste with salt and pepper and stir in the flaked almonds.

Beat the eggs in a bowl with the parsley, water, and salt and pepper to taste. Pour the mixture into the pan and cook for 5–8 minutes, or until the underside is set. Lift the edge of the tortilla occasionally to allow the uncooked egg to run underneath. Meanwhile, preheat the grill to high.

Sprinkle the grated cheese over the tortilla and cook under the preheated hot grill for 3 minutes, or until the top is set and the cheese has melted. Serve, lukewarm or cold, cut into thin wedges.

SERVES 4
as part of a tapas meal

2 tbsp Spanish olive oil

3 shallots, finely chopped

350 g/12 oz mushrooms, sliced

280 g/10 oz fresh spinach leaves, coarse stalks removed

55 g/2 oz toasted flaked almonds

5 eggs

2 tbsp chopped fresh parsley

2 tbsp cold water

85 g/3 oz mature Mahón, Manchego or Parmesan cheese, grated

salt and pepper

CHEESE & SHALLOTS WITH HERB DRESSING

**SERVES 6
as part of a tapas
meal**

1 tsp sesame seeds

1/4 tsp cumin seeds

4 tomatoes, deseeded
and diced

5 tbsp olive oil

4 tbsp lemon juice

2 tsp chopped fresh
thyme

1 tbsp chopped fresh
mint

4 shallots,
finely chopped

500 g/1 lb 2 oz Idiazabal
or other sheep's milk
cheese, diced

salt and pepper

Dry-fry the sesame and cumin seeds in a small, heavy-based frying pan, shaking the pan frequently, until they begin to pop and give off their aroma. Remove the frying pan from the heat and leave to cool.

Place the tomatoes in a bowl. To make the dressing, whisk the olive oil and lemon juice together in a separate bowl. Season to taste with salt and pepper, then add the thyme, mint and shallots and mix well.

Place the cheese in another bowl. Pour half the dressing over the tomatoes, then toss lightly, cover with clingfilm and leave to chill for 1 hour. Pour the remaining dressing over the cheese, cover and chill for 1 hour.

To serve, divide the cheese mixture between six serving plates and sprinkle with half the toasted seeds. Top with the tomato mixture and sprinkle with the remaining toasted seeds.

STUFFED EGGS

Cut the eggs in half lengthways and, using a teaspoon, carefully scoop out the yolks into a fine sieve, reserving the egg white halves. Rub the yolks through the sieve into a bowl.

Mash the sardines with a fork, then mix with the egg yolks. Stir in the lemon juice and Tabasco, then add enough mayonnaise to make a paste. Season to taste with salt and pepper.

Spoon the filling into the egg white halves, mounding it up well. Spread out the flour and breadcrumbs in separate shallow dishes. Dip each egg half first in the flour, then in the beaten egg and finally in the breadcrumbs.

Heat the oil for deep-frying in a deep-fat fryer or large saucepan to 180–190°C/ 350–375°F, or until a cube of bread browns in 30 seconds. Deep-fry the egg halves, in batches if necessary, for 2 minutes, or until golden brown. Drain on kitchen paper and serve hot, garnished with parsley sprigs.

**SERVES 6
as part of a tapas
meal**

6 hard-boiled eggs,
cooled and shelled

120 g/4$^1/_4$ oz canned
sardines in olive oil,
drained

4 tbsp lemon juice

dash of Tabasco sauce

1–2 tbsp mayonnaise

55 g/2 oz plain flour

85 g/3 oz fresh white
breadcrumbs

1 large egg,
lightly beaten

vegetable oil,
for deep-frying

salt and pepper

fresh parsley sprigs,
to garnish

OVEN-BAKED TORTILLA

MAKES 48 PIECES

3-4 tbsp Spanish olive oil

1 large garlic clove, crushed

4 spring onions, white and green parts finely chopped

1 green pepper, deseeded and finely diced

1 red pepper, deseeded and finely diced

175 g/6 oz potato, boiled, peeled and diced

5 large eggs

100 ml/3¹/₂ fl oz soured cream

175 g/6 oz freshly grated Spanish Roncal cheese, or Cheddar or Parmesan cheese

3 tbsp snipped fresh chives

salt and pepper

green salad, to serve

Preheat the oven to 190°C/375°F/Gas Mark 5. Line an 18 x 25-cm/7 x 10-inch baking tray with foil and brush with olive oil. Reserve.

Place the remaining olive oil, the garlic, spring onions and peppers in a frying pan. Cook over a medium heat, stirring, for 10 minutes, or until the onions are softened but not browned. Leave to cool, then stir in the potato.

Beat the eggs, soured cream, cheese and chives together in a large bowl. Stir the cooled vegetables into the egg mixture and season to taste with salt and pepper.

Pour the mixture into the baking tray and smooth over the top. Bake in the preheated oven for 30–40 minutes, or until golden brown, puffed and set in the centre. Remove from the oven and leave to cool and set. Run a spatula around the edge, then invert onto a chopping board, browned-side up, and peel off the foil. If the surface looks a little runny, place it under a medium grill to dry out.

Leave to cool completely. Trim the edges if necessary, then cut into 48 squares. Serve on a platter with wooden cocktail sticks, or secure each square to a slice of bread, and accompany with green salad.

FLAMENCO EGGS

Preheat the oven to 180°C/350°F/Gas Mark 4. Heat the olive oil in a large, heavy-based frying pan. Add the onion and garlic and cook over a low heat, stirring occasionally, for 5 minutes, or until softened. Add the red peppers and cook, stirring occasionally, for a further 10 minutes. Stir in the tomatoes and parsley, season to taste with salt and cayenne pepper and cook for a further 5 minutes.

Stir in the sweetcorn and remove the frying pan from the heat.

Divide the mixture between 4 individual ovenproof dishes. Make a hollow in the surface of each using the back of a large spoon. Break an egg into each depression.

Bake in the preheated oven for 15–25 minutes, or until the eggs have set. Serve hot.

**SERVES 4
as part of a tapas
meal**

4 tbsp olive oil

1 onion, thinly sliced

2 garlic cloves,
finely chopped

2 small red peppers,
deseeded and chopped

4 tomatoes, peeled,
deseeded and chopped

1 tbsp chopped fresh
parsley

200 g/7 oz canned
sweetcorn kernels,
drained

4 eggs

salt and cayenne pepper

The Baker's Choice

GARLIC FRIED BREAD & CHORIZO

SERVES 6–8
as part of a tapas
meal

200 g/7 oz chorizo
sausage, outer casing
removed

4 thick slices 2-day-old
country bread

Spanish olive oil, for
shallow-frying

3 garlic cloves,
finely chopped

2 tbsp chopped fresh
flat-leaf parsley

paprika, to garnish

Cut the chorizo sausage into 1-cm/½-inch thick slices and cut the bread, with its crusts still on, into 1-cm/½-inch cubes. Add sufficient olive oil to a large, heavy-based frying pan so that it generously covers the base. Heat the oil, add the garlic and fry for 30–60 seconds, or until lightly browned.

Add the bread cubes to the pan and fry, stirring all the time, until golden brown and crisp. Add the chorizo slices and fry for

1–2 minutes, or until hot. Using a slotted spoon, remove the bread cubes and chorizo from the pan and drain well on kitchen paper.

Turn the fried bread and chorizo into a warmed serving bowl, add the chopped parsley and toss together. Garnish the dish with a sprinkling of paprika and serve warm. Accompany with cocktail sticks so that a piece of sausage and a cube of bread can be speared together for eating.

CHORIZO EMPANADILLAS

Preheat the oven to 200°C/400°F/Gas Mark 6. Cut the chorizo sausage into small cubes measuring about 1 cm/½ inch square.

On a lightly floured work surface, thinly roll out the puff pastry. Using a plain, round 8-cm/3¼-inch cutter, cut into rounds. Gently pile the trimmings together, roll out again, then cut out further rounds to produce 12 in total. Put about a teaspoon of the chopped chorizo on to each of the pastry rounds.

Dampen the edges of the pastry with a little water, then fold one half over the other half to cover the chorizo completely. Seal the edges together with your fingers. Using the prongs of a fork, press against the edges to give a decorative finish and seal them further. With the tip of a sharp knife, make a small slit in the side of each pastry. You can store the pastries in the refrigerator at this stage until you are ready to bake them.

Place the pastries onto dampened baking trays and brush each with a little beaten egg to glaze. Bake in the oven for 10–15 minutes, or until golden brown and puffed. Using a small sieve, lightly dust the top of each empanadilla with a little paprika to garnish. Serve the chorizo empanadillas hot or warm.

MAKES 12

125 g/4½ oz chorizo sausage, outer casing removed

plain flour, for dusting

250 g/9 oz ready-made puff pastry, thawed if frozen

beaten egg, to glaze

paprika, to garnish

CHEESE & HAM PASTRIES

Preheat the oven to 200°C/400°F/Gas Mark 6. Spread out the ham and brush with Tabasco to taste. Cut the cheese into six slices. Wrap a slice of cheese in each slice of ham.

Working on one sheet of filo dough at a time and keeping the others covered with a clean, damp tea towel, brush with a little olive oil, then fold in half. Place one ham-wrapped slice of cheese in the centre, brush the filo pastry with oil again and fold it over to enclose the cheese completely. Place on a baking sheet, seam-side down, and brush the top with a little oil. Repeat with the remaining sheets of filo and ham-wrapped cheese.

Bake in the preheated oven for 15 minutes, or until golden brown and crisp. Serve immediately or leave to cool slightly and serve warm.

MAKES 6

6 slices serrano ham

Tabasco sauce, for brushing

200 g/7 oz Queso Majorero, Manchego or goat's cheese

6 sheets filo pastry, about 46 x 28 cm/ 18 x 11 inches

3–4 tbsp Spanish olive oil

CRAB TARTLETS

Preheat the oven to 190ºC/375ºF/Gas Mark 5. To prepare the crabmeat filling, heat the olive oil in a saucepan, add the onion and fry for 5 minutes, or until softened but not browned. Add the garlic and fry for a further 30 seconds. Add a splash of wine and cook for 1–2 minutes, or until most of the wine has evaporated.

Lightly whisk the eggs in a large mixing bowl, then whisk in the milk or cream. Add the crabmeat, cheese and parsley, and the onion mixture. Season the mixture with nutmeg, and salt and pepper to taste, and mix well together.

To prepare the pastry if you are making it yourself, mix the flour and salt together in a large mixing bowl. Add the butter, cut into small pieces, and rub in until the mixture resembles fine breadcrumbs. Gradually stir in enough of the water to form a firm dough. Alternatively, the pastry could be made in a food processor.

On a lightly floured work surface, thinly roll out the pastry. Using a plain, round 7-cm/2³/4-inch cutter, cut the pastry into 18 rounds. Gently pile the trimmings together, roll out again, then cut out a further 6 rounds. Use to line 24 tartlet tins measuring 4 cm/1¹/2 inch Carefully spoon the crabmeat mixture into the pastry cases, taking care not to overfill them.

Bake the tartlets in the oven for 25–30 minutes, or until golden brown and set. Serve the crab tartlets hot or cold, garnished with fresh dill sprigs.

MAKES 24

1 tbsp Spanish olive oil

1 small onion, finely chopped

1 garlic clove, finely chopped

splash of dry white wine

2 eggs

150 ml/5 fl oz milk or single cream

175 g/6 oz canned crabmeat, drained

55 g/2 oz Manchego or Parmesan cheese, grated

2 tbsp chopped fresh flat-leaf parsley

pinch of freshly grated nutmeg

salt and pepper

sprigs of fresh dill, to garnish

PASTRY

350 g/12 oz plain flour, plus extra for dusting

pinch of salt

175 g/6 oz butter

2 tbsp cold water

OR

500 g/1 lb 2 oz ready-made shortcrust pastry

SPANISH SPINACH & TOMATO PIZZAS

MAKES 32

2 tbsp Spanish olive oil, plus extra for brushing and drizzling

1 onion, finely chopped

1 garlic clove, finely chopped

400 g/14 oz canned chopped tomatoes

125 g/4^1/$_2$ oz baby spinach leaves

4 tbsp pine kernels

salt and pepper

BREAD DOUGH

100 ml/3^1/$_2$ fl oz warm water

^{1}/$_2$ tsp easy-blend dried yeast

pinch of sugar

200 g/7 oz strong white flour, plus extra for dusting

^{1}/$_2$ tsp salt

To make the bread dough, measure the water into a small bowl, sprinkle in the dried yeast and sugar and leave in a warm place for 10–15 minutes, or until frothy.

Meanwhile, sift the flour and salt into a large bowl. Make a well in the centre of the flour and pour in the yeast liquid, then mix together with a wooden spoon. Using your hands, work the mixture until it leaves the sides of the bowl clean.

Turn the dough out on to a lightly floured work surface and knead for 10 minutes, or until smooth and elastic and no longer sticky. Shape into a ball and put it in a clean bowl. Cover with a clean, damp tea towel and leave in a warm place for 1 hour, or until the dough has risen and doubled in size.

To make the topping, heat the olive oil in a large, heavy-based frying pan. Add the onion and fry for 5 minutes, or until softened but not browned. Add the garlic and fry for a further 30 seconds. Stir in the tomatoes and cook for 5 minutes, letting it bubble and stirring occasionally, until reduced to a thick mixture. Add the spinach leaves and cook, stirring, until they have wilted a little. Season the mixture to taste with salt and pepper.

While the dough is rising, preheat the oven to 200°C/400°F/Gas Mark 6. Brush several baking trays with olive oil. Turn the dough out on to a lightly floured work surface and knead well for 2–3 minutes to knock out the air bubbles. Roll out the dough very, very thinly and, using a 6-cm/2^1/$_2$-inch plain, round cutter, cut out 32 rounds. Place on the prepared baking sheets.

Spread each base with the spinach mixture to cover, then sprinkle the pine kernels over the top. Drizzle a little olive oil over each pizza. Bake in the oven for 10–15 minutes, or until the edges of the dough are golden brown. Serve the spinach and tomato pizzas hot.

ANCHOVY ROLLS

Preheat the oven to 220°C/425°F/Gas Mark 7. Lightly grease a baking sheet. Place the anchovies in a small, shallow dish and pour over the milk. Leave to soak for 10–15 minutes. Drain, discarding the milk, and pat dry with kitchen paper.

Spread each bread slice with butter and then with mustard. Sprinkle with the grated cheese. Divide the anchovy between the bread slices and roll up.

Place on the baking sheet, seam-side down, and bake in the preheated oven for 6–7 minutes. Leave to cool slightly, then serve.

MAKES 4

butter, for greasing and spreading

8 salted anchovies, filleted

50 ml/2 fl oz milk

4 slices white bread, crusts removed

1 tbsp Dijon mustard

2 tbsp grated Manchego or Cheddar cheese

CHORIZO & QUAIL EGGS

MAKES 12

12 slices French bread, sliced diagonally, about 5 mm/¼ inch thick

40 g/1½ oz cured, ready-to-eat chorizo, cut into 12 thin slices

olive oil, for frying

12 quail eggs

mild paprika, for dusting

salt and pepper

fresh flat-leaf parsley, to garnish

Preheat the grill to high. Arrange the slices of bread on a baking sheet and grill until golden brown on both sides.

Cut or fold the chorizo slices to fit on the toasts, then reserve.

Heat a thin layer of olive oil in a large frying pan over a medium heat until a cube of bread browns — about 40 seconds. Break the eggs into the frying pan and fry, spooning the fat over the yolks, until the whites are set and the yolks are cooked to your liking.

Remove the fried eggs from the frying pan and drain on kitchen paper. Immediately transfer to the chorizo-topped toasts and dust with paprika. Season to taste with salt and pepper, garnish with parsley and serve immediately.

CHEESE & OLIVE EMPANADILLAS

Preheat the oven to 200°C/400°F/Gas Mark 6. Cut the cheese into small cubes measuring about 5 mm/¼ inch. Chop the olives, sun-dried tomatoes and anchovies into pieces about the same size as the cheese. Put all the chopped ingredients in a bowl, season with pepper to taste and gently mix together. Stir in the sun-dried tomato purée.

On a lightly floured work surface, thinly roll out the puff pastry. Using a plain, round 8-cm/3¼-inch cutter, cut into 18 rounds. Gently pile the trimmings together, roll out again, then cut out a further 8 rounds. Using a teaspoon, put a little of the prepared filling equally in the centre of each of the pastry rounds.

Dampen the edges of the pastry with a little water, then bring up the sides to cover the filling completely and pinch the edges together with your fingers to seal them. With the tip of a sharp knife, make a small slit in the top of each pastry. You can store the pastries in the refrigerator at this stage until you are ready to bake them.

Place the pastries on to dampened baking trays and brush each with a little beaten egg to glaze. Bake in the oven for 10–15 minutes, or until golden brown, crisp and well risen. Serve the empanadillas piping hot, warm or cold and garnish with parsley.

MAKES 26

85 g/3 oz firm or
soft cheese

85 g/3 oz stoned
green olives

55 g/2 oz sun-dried
tomatoes in oil, drained

50 g/1¾ oz canned
anchovy fillets, drained

pepper

55 g/2 oz sun-dried
tomato purée

plain flour, for dusting

500 g/1 lb 2 oz
ready-made puff pastry,
thawed if frozen

beaten egg, to glaze

fresh flat-leaf
parsley, to garnish

FLATBREAD WITH VEGETABLES & CLAMS

**SERVES 4–6
as part of a tapas
meal**

2 tbsp Spanish extra
virgin olive oil

4 large garlic cloves,
crushed

2 large onions,
thinly sliced

10 pimientos del
piquillo, drained, patted
dry and thinly sliced

250 g/9 oz shelled
baby clams in brine
(weight in jar), drained
and rinsed

salt and pepper

DOUGH

400 g/14 oz strong
white flour,
plus extra for dusting

1 sachet easy-blend
dried yeast

1 tsp salt

$1/2$ tsp sugar

1 tbsp olive oil, plus
extra for oiling

1 tbsp dry white wine

225 ml/8 fl oz warm
water

To make the dough, stir the flour, yeast, salt and sugar together in a bowl, making a well in the centre. Add the olive oil and wine to the water, then pour 175 ml/6 fl oz of the liquid into the well. Gradually mix in the flour from the sides, adding the remaining liquid if necessary, until a soft dough forms.

Turn out the dough onto a lightly floured surface and knead until smooth. Shape the dough into a ball. Wash the bowl and rub the inside with olive oil. Return the dough to the bowl and roll it around so that it is lightly coated in oil. Cover the bowl tightly with clingfilm and leave in a warm place until the dough doubles in size.

Heat the olive oil in a large, heavy-based frying pan over a medium heat. Reduce the heat and add the garlic and onions and fry slowly, stirring frequently, for 25 minutes, or until the onions are golden brown but not burned.

Preheat the oven to 230°C/450°F/ Gas Mark 8. Transfer the onions to a bowl and leave to cool. Add the pepper strips and clams to the bowl and stir together. Reserve.

Knock back the dough and knead quickly on a lightly floured work surface. Cover it with the upturned bowl and leave for 10 minutes, which will make it easier to roll out.

Heavily flour a 32 x 32-cm/12^3/4 x 12^3/4-inch shallow baking tray. Roll out the dough to make a 34-cm/13^1/2-inch square and transfer it to the baking tray, rolling the edges to form a thin rim. Prick the base all over with a fork.

Spread the topping evenly over the dough and season to taste with salt and pepper. Bake in the preheated oven for 25 minutes, or until the rim is golden brown and the onions tips are slightly tinged. Transfer to a wire rack to cool completely. Cut into 12–16 slices.

ONION & OLIVE ROUNDS

Heat the olive oil in a heavy-based frying pan. Add the onion and garlic and cook over a low heat, stirring occasionally, for 15 minutes, or until golden brown and very soft. Stir in the thyme and season to taste with salt and pepper.

Meanwhile, cut off and discard the crusty ends of the bread, then cut the loaf into eight slices. Toast on both sides, then spread with tapenade or butter.

Pile the onion mixture on to the slices of toast and top each slice with an anchovy fillet and the olives. Serve hot.

SERVES 4–8
as part of a tapas
meal

2 tbsp olive oil

1 onion, thinly sliced

1 garlic clove,
finely chopped

2 tsp chopped fresh
thyme

1 small loaf of French
bread

1 tbsp tapenade or
butter

8 canned anchovy
fillets in oil, drained

12 olives stuffed with
almonds or onion,
halved

salt and pepper

PRAWN & HARICOT TOASTS

Halve one of the garlic cloves and reserve. Finely chop the remaining cloves. Heat two tablespoons of the olive oil in a large, heavy-based frying pan. Add the chopped garlic and onion and cook over a low heat, stirring occasionally, for 5 minutes, or until softened.

Stir in the beans and tomatoes and season to taste with salt and pepper. Cook gently for a further 5 minutes.

Meanwhile, toast the bread on both sides, then rub each slice with the cut sides of the reserved garlic and drizzle with the remaining oil.

Stir the prawns into the bean mixture and heat through gently for 2–3 minutes. Pile the bean and prawn mixture onto the toasts and serve immediately, garnished with watercress.

SERVES 4

3 garlic cloves

4 tbsp olive oil

1 Spanish onion, halved and finely chopped

400 g/14 oz canned haricot beans, drained and rinsed

4 tomatoes, diced

4 thick slices country bread

280 g/10 oz cooked peeled prawns

salt and pepper

watercress, to garnish

OLIVE & RED PEPPER BREAD

Preheat the grill to high. Place the pepper halves, skin-side up, in a single layer on a baking sheet. Cook under the hot grill for 8–10 minutes, or until the skin is blackened and blistered all over. Using tongs, transfer to a polythene bag, tie the top and leave to cool. When cool enough to handle, peel off the skin.

Finely chop one of the garlic cloves. Place in a food processor or blender with the pepper halves, capers, parsley, lemon juice, cumin and sugar and process until smooth. Scrape into a bowl and stir in the olives.

Cut off and discard the crusty ends of the bread, then cut the bread into 1-cm/½-inch slices. Toast the slices on both sides. Cut the remaining garlic cloves in half, then rub the cut sides all over the toast. Brush the toast with the olive oil.

Spoon the red pepper mixture onto the toasted bread and place on a large serving platter. Serve immediately.

SERVES 4–6 as part of a tapas meal

2 red peppers, halved and deseeded

3 garlic cloves

2 tsp capers, drained, rinsed and halved

4 tbsp chopped fresh parsley

1 tbsp lemon juice

1 tsp ground cumin

2 tsp sugar

55 g/2 oz black olives, stoned and chopped

1 loaf of French bread

2 tbsp olive oil

ASPARAGUS ROLLS

MAKES 8

115 g/4 oz butter, softened, plus extra for greasing

8 asparagus spears, trimmed

8 slices white bread, crusts removed

1 tbsp chopped fresh parsley

finely grated rind of 1 orange

salt and pepper

Preheat the oven to 190°C/375°F/Gas Mark 5 and lightly grease a baking sheet. If woody, peel the asparagus stems, then tie the spears loosely together with clean kitchen string. Blanch in a tall saucepan of boiling water for 3–5 minutes. Drain and refresh under cold running water. Drain again and pat dry with kitchen paper.

Lightly flatten the slices of bread with a rolling pin. Mix 70 g/2½ oz of the butter, the parsley and orange rind together in a bowl and season to taste with salt and pepper.

Spread the flavoured butter over the bread slices.

Place an asparagus spear near one side of a bread slice and roll up. Repeat with the remaining asparagus spears and bread. Place the asparagus rolls, seam-side down, on the baking sheet.

Melt the remaining butter in a small saucepan, then brush it over the asparagus rolls. Bake in the preheated oven for 15 minutes, or until crisp and golden brown. Leave to cool slightly, then serve warm.

TOMATO TOASTS WITH THREE TOPPINGS

Toast the bread on both sides. Meanwhile, place the diced tomato in a bowl and mix in the garlic. Spread the tomato mixture evenly over the toast, season to taste with salt and pepper and drizzle with the olive oil.

For the ham and caper topping, arrange the strips of ham in an 'S' shape across four of the toasts and place a caper in the curves of each letter 'S'.

For the chorizo and cheese topping, place two slices of chorizo on each of four of the remaining toasts and top with the cheese. Garnish with an olive half.

For the anchovy and olive topping, curl three anchovy fillets into circles, place on each of the remaining four toasts and put an olive in the centre of each.

SERVES 4–6

12 thick slices country bread

12 tomatoes, peeled, deseeded and diced

8 garlic cloves, finely chopped

about 350 ml/12 fl oz olive oil

salt and pepper

HAM & CAPER TOPPING

2 slices ham, cut into thin strips

8 capers, drained and rinsed

CHORIZO & CHEESE TOPPING

8 slices ready-to-eat chorizo sausage

55 g/2 oz Manchego or Cheddar cheese, sliced

2 pimiento-stuffed olives, halved

ANCHOVY & OLIVE TOPPING

12 canned anchovy fillets in oil, drained

4 anchovy-stuffed green olives

Fish & Meat Morsels

SIZZLING CHILLI PRAWNS

**SERVES 8
as part of a tapas
meal**

500 g/1 lb 2 oz raw
tiger prawns
in their shells

1 small fresh red chilli

6 tbsp Spanish olive oil

2 garlic cloves,
finely chopped

pinch of paprika

salt

crusty bread, to serve

To prepare the prawns, pull off their heads. With your fingers, peel off their shells, leaving the tails intact. Using a sharp knife, make a shallow slit along the back of each prawn, then pull out the dark vein and discard. Rinse the prawns under cold water and dry well on kitchen paper.

Cut the chilli in half lengthways, remove the seeds and finely chop the flesh. Heat the oil in a large, heavy-based frying pan or flameproof casserole until quite hot, then add the garlic and fry for 30 seconds. Add the prawns, chilli, paprika and a pinch of salt and fry for 2-3 minutes, stirring all the time, until the prawns turn pink and begin to curl.

Serve the prawns in the cooking dish, still sizzling. Accompany with cocktail sticks, to spear the prawns, and chunks or slices of crusty bread to mop up the aromatic cooking oil.

MINIATURE PORK BROCHETTES

The brochettes are marinated overnight, so remember to do this in advance in order that they are ready when you need them. Cut the pork into pieces about 2 cm/³/₄ inch square and put in a large, shallow, non-metallic dish that will hold the pieces in a single layer.

To prepare the marinade, put all the remaining ingredients in a non-metallic bowl and mix well together. Pour the marinade over the pork and toss the meat in it until well coated. Cover the dish and leave to marinate in the refrigerator for 8 hours or overnight, stirring the pork 2–3 times.

You can use wooden or metal skewers to cook the brochettes and for this recipe you will need about twelve 15-cm/6-inch skewers.

If you are using wooden ones, soak them in cold water for about 30 minutes prior to using. This helps to stop them burning and the food sticking to them during cooking. Metal skewers simply need to be greased, and flat ones should be used in preference to round ones to prevent the food on them falling off.

Preheat the grill, griddle or barbecue. Thread about three marinated pork pieces, leaving a little space between each piece, on to each prepared skewer. Cook the brochettes for 10–15 minutes or until tender and lightly charred, turning several times and basting with the remaining marinade during cooking. Serve the pork brochettes piping hot, garnished with parsley and accompanied by stuffed olives.

MAKES 12

450 g/1 lb lean boneless pork

3 tbsp Spanish olive oil, plus extra for oiling (optional)

grated rind and juice of 1 large lemon

2 garlic cloves, crushed

2 tbsp chopped fresh flat-leaf parsley, plus extra to garnish

1 tbsp ras-el-hanout Moroccan spice blend

salt and pepper

stuffed olives, to serve

COD & CAPER CROQUETTES

MAKES 12

350 g/12 oz white fish fillets, such as cod, haddock or monkfish

300 ml/10 fl oz milk

4 tbsp Spanish olive oil or 55 g/2 oz butter

55 g/2 oz plain flour

4 tbsp capers, roughly chopped

1 tsp paprika, plus extra for dusting

1 garlic clove, crushed

1 tsp lemon juice

3 tbsp chopped fresh flat-leaf parsley, plus extra sprigs to garnish

1 egg, beaten

55 g/2 oz fresh white breadcrumbs

1 tbsp sesame seeds

groundnut oil, for deep-frying

salt and pepper

lemon wedges, to garnish

mayonnaise, to serve

Put the fish fillets in a large, heavy-based frying pan. Pour in the milk and season to taste with salt and pepper. Bring to the boil, then reduce the heat, cover the pan and simmer gently for 8–10 minutes, or until the fish flakes easily when tested with a fork. Using a fish slice, remove the fish fillets from the pan. Pour the milk into a jug and reserve for later. Flake the fish, removing and discarding the skin and bones.

Heat the olive oil in a saucepan. Stir in the flour to form a paste and cook gently, stirring, for 1 minute. Remove the saucepan from the heat and gradually stir in the reserved milk until smooth. Return to the heat and slowly bring to the boil, stirring all the time, until the mixture thickens.

Remove the saucepan from the heat, add the flaked fish and beat until the mixture is smooth. Add the capers, paprika, garlic, lemon juice and parsley and mix well together. Season the mixture to taste with salt and pepper. Spread the fish mixture in a dish and

leave until cool, then cover and put in the refrigerator for 2–3 hours or overnight.

When the fish mixture has chilled, pour the beaten egg onto a plate. Put the breadcrumbs and sesame seeds on a separate plate, mix together and spread out. Divide the fish mixture into 12 equal-sized portions. Then, with lightly floured hands, form each portion into a sausage shape, measuring about 7.5 cm/ 3 inches in length. Dip the croquettes, one at a time, in the beaten egg, then roll in the breadcrumb mixture to coat them. Place on a plate, cover and chill for about 1 hour.

To cook the croquettes, heat the groundnut oil in a deep fryer to 180–190°C/350–375°F, or until a cube of bread browns in 30 seconds. Add the croquettes, in batches, and fry for 3 minutes, or until golden brown and crispy. Remove from the pan with a slotted spoon and drain well on kitchen paper.

Serve piping hot, garnished with lemon wedges and parsley sprigs and accompanied by mayonnaise dusted with paprika for dipping.

CHICKEN IN LEMON & GARLIC

Using a sharp knife, slice the chicken breasts widthways into very thin slices. Heat the olive oil in a large, heavy-based frying pan, add the onion and fry for 5 minutes, or until softened but not browned. Add the garlic and fry for a further 30 seconds.

Add the sliced chicken to the pan and fry gently for 5–10 minutes, stirring from time to time, until all the ingredients are lightly browned and the chicken is cooked through.

Add the grated lemon rind and the lemon juice and let it bubble. At the same time, deglaze the pan by scraping and stirring all the bits on the base of the pan into the juices with a wooden spoon. Remove the pan from the heat, stir in the parsley and season to taste with salt and pepper.

Transfer the chicken in lemon and garlic, piping hot, to a warmed serving platter. Sprinkle with the pared lemon rind, garnish with the parsley and serve with lemon wedges for squeezing over the chicken.

**SERVES 6–8
as part of a tapas
meal**

4 large skinless,
boneless chicken
breasts

5 tbsp Spanish olive oil

1 onion, finely chopped

6 garlic cloves,
finely chopped

grated rind of 1 lemon,
finely pared rind of
1 lemon and juice of
both lemons

4 tbsp chopped fresh
flat-leaf parsley,
plus extra sprigs
to garnish

salt and pepper

lemon wedges, to
serve

CALAMARES

**SERVES 6
as part of a tapas
meal**

450 g/1 lb prepared
squid

plain flour, for coating

groundnut oil,
for deep-frying

salt

lemon wedges,
to garnish

aïoli (see page 164),
to serve

Slice the squid into 1-cm/½-inch rings and halve the tentacles if large. Rinse and dry well on kitchen paper so that they do not spit during cooking. Dust the squid rings with flour so that they are lightly coated. Do not season the flour: Spanish cooks will tell you that seasoning squid with salt before cooking toughens it.

Heat the groundnut oil in a deep fryer to 180–190°C/350–375°F, or until a cube of bread browns in 30 seconds. Carefully add the squid rings, in batches so that the temperature of the oil does not drop, and fry for 2–3 minutes, or until golden brown and crisp all over, turning several times. Do not overcook because the squid will become tough and rubbery rather than moist and tender.

Using a slotted spoon, remove the fried squid from the deep fryer and drain well on kitchen paper. Keep warm in a warm oven while you fry the remaining squid rings.

Sprinkle the fried squid rings with salt and serve piping hot, garnished with lemon wedges for squeezing over them. Accompany with a bowl of aïoli in which to dip the calamares.

CRISPY CHICKEN & HAM CROQUETTES

Heat the olive oil or butter in a saucepan. Stir in the flour to form a paste and cook gently for 1 minute, stirring constantly. Remove the saucepan from the heat and gradually stir in the milk until smooth. Return to the heat and slowly bring to the boil, stirring all the time, until the mixture boils and thickens.

Remove the saucepan from the heat, add the minced chicken and beat until the mixture is smooth. Add the chopped ham, parsley and nutmeg and mix well together. Season the mixture to taste with salt and pepper. Spread the chicken mixture in a dish and leave for 30 minutes until cool, then cover and put in the refrigerator for 2–3 hours or overnight. Don't be tempted to miss out this stage, because chilling helps to stop the croquettes from falling apart when they are cooked.

When the chicken mixture has chilled, pour the beaten egg onto a plate and spread the breadcrumbs out on a separate plate. Divide the chicken mixture into 8 equal-sized portions. With dampened hands, form each portion into a cylindrical shape. Dip the croquettes, one at a time, in the beaten egg, then roll in the breadcrumbs to coat them. Place on a plate and chill in the refrigerator for about 1 hour.

To cook the croquettes, heat the oil in a deep fryer to 180–190°C/350–375°F, or until a cube of bread browns in 30 seconds. Add the croquettes, in batches to prevent the temperature of the oil from dropping, and fry for 5–10 minutes, or until golden brown and crispy. Remove from the pan with a slotted spoon and drain well on kitchen paper.

Serve the chicken and ham croquettes piping hot, garnished with parsley sprigs and accompanied by a bowl of aïoli for dipping.

MAKES 8

4 tbsp Spanish olive oil or 55 g/2 oz butter

4 tbsp plain flour

200 ml/7 fl oz milk

115 g/4 oz cooked chicken, minced

55 g/2 oz serrano or cooked ham, very finely chopped

1 tbsp chopped fresh flat-leaf parsley, plus extra sprigs to garnish

small pinch of freshly grated nutmeg

salt and pepper

1 egg, beaten

55 g/2 oz day-old white breadcrumbs

groundnut oil, for deep-frying

aïoli (see page 164), to serve

LIME-DRIZZLED PRAWNS

**SERVES 6
as part of a tapas
meal**

4 limes

12 raw king prawns,
in their shells

3 tbsp Spanish olive oil

2 garlic cloves,
finely chopped

splash of dry sherry

salt and pepper

4 tbsp chopped fresh
flat-leaf parsley

Grate the rind and squeeze out the juice from two of the limes. Cut the remaining two limes into wedges and reserve for later.

To prepare the prawns, remove the heads and legs, leaving the shells and tails intact. Using a sharp knife, make a shallow slit along the back of each prawn, then pull out the dark vein and discard. Rinse the prawns under cold water and dry well on kitchen paper.

Heat the olive oil in a large, heavy-based frying pan, then add the garlic and fry for 30 seconds. Add the prawns and fry for 5 minutes, stirring from time to time, or until they turn pink and begin to curl. Mix in the lime rind, juice and a splash of sherry to moisten, then stir well together.

Transfer the cooked prawns to a serving dish, season to taste with salt and pepper and sprinkle over the parsley. Serve piping hot, accompanied by the reserved lime wedges for squeezing over the prawns.

BROAD BEANS WITH SERRANO HAM

Using a sharp knife, cut the ham, pancetta or bacon into small strips. Cut the chorizo into 2-cm/³⁄₄-inch cubes. Heat the olive oil in a large, heavy-based frying pan or flameproof dish that has a lid. Add the onion and fry for 5 minutes, or until softened and beginning to brown. If you are using pancetta or bacon, add it with the onion. Add the garlic and fry for a further 30 seconds.

Pour the wine into the pan, increase the heat and let it bubble to evaporate the alcohol, then reduce the heat. Add the broad beans, ham if using, and the chorizo and fry for 1–2 minutes, stirring all the time to coat in the oil.

Cover the pan and let the beans simmer very gently in the oil, stirring from time to time, for 10–15 minutes, or until the beans are tender. It may be necessary to add a little water to the pan during cooking, so keep an eye on it and add a splash if the beans appear to become too dry. Stir in the mint and the sugar. Season the dish with salt and pepper, but taste first because you may find that it does not need any salt.

Transfer the broad beans to a large, warmed serving dish, several smaller ones or individual plates and serve piping hot, garnished with chopped mint.

**SERVES 6–8
as part of a tapas
meal**

55 g/2 oz serrano ham, Parma ham, pancetta or rindless smoked streaky bacon

115 g/4 oz chorizo sausage, outer casing removed

4 tbsp Spanish olive oil

1 onion, finely chopped

2 garlic cloves, finely chopped

splash of dry white wine

450 g/1 lb frozen broad beans, thawed, or about 1.3 kg/3 lb fresh broad beans in their pods, shelled to give 450 g/1 lb

1 tbsp chopped fresh mint or dill, plus extra to garnish

pinch of sugar

salt and pepper

TUNA WITH PIMIENTO-STUFFED OLIVES

SERVES 6
as part of a tapas meal

2 fresh tuna steaks,
weighing about
250 g/9 oz in total and
about 2.5 cm/1 inch thick

5 tbsp Spanish olive oil

3 tbsp red wine vinegar

4 sprigs of fresh thyme,
plus extra to garnish

1 bay leaf

salt and pepper

2 tbsp plain flour

1 onion, finely chopped

2 garlic cloves,
finely chopped

85 g/3 oz pimiento-stuffed
green olives, sliced

lemon wedges, to garnish

crusty bread, to serve

Prepare this dish the day before you are going to serve it. Remove any skin from the tuna steaks, then cut the steaks in half along the grain of the fish. Cut each half into 1-cm/½-inch thick slices against the grain.

Put three tablespoons of the olive oil and the vinegar in a large, shallow, non-metallic dish. Strip the leaves from the sprigs of thyme and add these to the dish with the bay leaf and salt and pepper to taste. Add the prepared strips of tuna, cover the dish and leave to marinate in the refrigerator for 8 hours or overnight.

The next day, put the flour in a polythene bag. Remove the tuna strips from the marinade, reserving the marinade for later, add them to the bag of flour and toss well until they are lightly coated.

Heat the remaining olive oil in a large, heavy-based frying pan. Add the onion and garlic and gently fry for 5–10 minutes, or until softened and golden brown. Add the tuna strips to the pan and fry for 2–5 minutes, turning several times, until the fish becomes opaque. Add the reserved marinade and olives to the pan and cook for a further 1–2 minutes, stirring, until the fish is tender and the sauce has thickened.

Serve the tuna and olives piping hot, garnished with thyme sprigs and lemon wedges. Accompany with chunks or slices of crusty bread for mopping up the sauce.

ROASTED ASPARAGUS WITH MOUNTAIN HAM

Preheat the oven to 200°C/400°F/Gas Mark 6. Put half the olive oil in a roasting tin that will hold the asparagus spears in a single layer and swirl it around so that it covers the base. Cut each slice of serrano ham in half lengthways.

Trim the ends of the asparagus spears, then wrap a slice of ham around the stem end of each spear. Place the wrapped spears in the prepared roasting tin and lightly brush the ham and asparagus with the remaining olive oil. Season the spears with pepper.

Roast the asparagus spears in the oven for about 10 minutes, depending on the thickness of the asparagus, until tender but still firm. Do not overcook the asparagus spears because it is important that they are still firm, so that you can pick them up with your fingers.

Serve the roasted asparagus with mountain ham piping hot, accompanied by a bowl of aïoli for dipping.

MAKES 12

2 tbsp Spanish olive oil

6 slices serrano ham

12 asparagus spears

pepper

aïoli (see page 164), to serve

MONKFISH, ROSEMARY & BACON SKEWERS

MAKES 12

350 g/12 oz monkfish tail or 250 g/9 oz monkfish fillet

12 long stalks of fresh rosemary

3 tbsp Spanish olive oil

juice of ¹/₂ small lemon

1 garlic clove, crushed

salt and pepper

6 thick back bacon rashers

lemon wedges, to garnish

aïoli (see page 164), to serve

If using monkfish tail, cut either side of the central bone with a sharp knife and remove the flesh to form 2 fillets. Slice the fillets in half lengthways, then cut each fillet into 12 bite-sized chunks to give a total of 24 pieces. Put the monkfish pieces in a large bowl.

To prepare the rosemary skewers, strip the leaves off the stalks and reserve them, leaving a few leaves at one end.

For the marinade, finely chop the reserved leaves and whisk together in a bowl with the olive oil, lemon juice, garlic, and salt and pepper to taste. Add the monkfish pieces and toss until coated in the marinade. Cover and leave to marinate in the refrigerator for 1–2 hours.

Cut each bacon rasher in half lengthways, then in half widthways, and roll up each piece.

Thread 2 pieces of monkfish alternately with 2 bacon rolls on to the prepared rosemary skewers.

Preheat the grill or griddle. If you are cooking the skewers under an overhead grill, arrange them on the grill pan so that the leaves of the rosemary skewers protrude from the grill and therefore do not catch fire during cooking. Grill the monkfish and bacon skewers for 10 minutes, turning from time to time and basting with any remaining marinade, or until cooked. Serve hot, garnished with lemon wedges for squeezing over them and accompanied by a bowl of aïoli in which to dip the monkfish skewers.

BEEF SKEWERS WITH ORANGE & GARLIC

Mix the wine, olive oil, garlic and orange juice together in a shallow, non-metallic dish. Add the cubes of steak, season to taste with salt and pepper and toss to coat. Cover with clingfilm and leave to marinate in the refrigerator for 2–8 hours.

Preheat the grill to high. Drain the steak, reserving the marinade. Thread the steak, onions, peppers and tomatoes alternately onto several small skewers.

Cook under the hot grill, turning and brushing frequently with the marinade, for 10 minutes, or until cooked through. Transfer to warmed serving plates and serve immediately.

SERVES 6–8
as part of a tapas meal

3 tbsp white wine

2 tbsp Spanish olive oil

3 garlic cloves, finely chopped

juice of 1 orange

450 g/1 lb rump steak, cubed

450 g/1 lb button onions, halved

2 orange peppers, deseeded and cut into squares

225 g/8 oz cherry tomatoes, halved

salt and pepper

DEEP-FRIED SARDINES

**SERVES 6–8
as part of a tapas
meal**

125 ml/4 fl oz red wine
vinegar

3 garlic cloves,
finely chopped

1 fresh red chilli,
deseeded and
finely chopped

2 tbsp chopped fresh
parsley

1 kg/2 lb 4 oz fresh
sardines, scaled,
cleaned and heads
removed

115 g/4 oz plain flour

vegetable oil,
for deep-frying

salt and pepper

lemon wedges,
to garnish

Mix the vinegar, garlic, chilli and parsley together in a large, non-metallic dish. Add the sardines, turn to coat, then cover with clingfilm and leave to marinate in the refrigerator for 1 hour.

Drain the sardines and pat dry with kitchen paper. Place the flour in a polythene bag, season to taste with salt and pepper and add the sardines, a few at a time, shaking to coat well.

Heat the vegetable oil in a deep fryer or large saucepan to 180–190°C/350–375°F, or until a cube of bread browns in 30 seconds. Deep-fry the sardines, in batches, for 4–5 minutes, or until golden brown. Remove and drain on kitchen paper. Keep warm while you cook the remaining sardines. Serve garnished with lemon wedges.

LAMB SKEWERS WITH LEMON

Mix the garlic, onion, lemon rind, lemon juice, thyme, coriander, cumin, vinegar and olive oil together in a large, shallow, non-metallic dish, whisking well until thoroughly combined.

Thread the pieces of lamb onto 16 wooden skewers and add to the dish, turning well to coat. Cover with clingfilm and leave to marinate in the refrigerator for 2–8 hours, turning occasionally.

Preheat the grill to medium. Drain the skewers, reserving the marinade. Cook under the hot grill, turning frequently and brushing with the marinade, for 10 minutes, or until tender and cooked to your liking. Serve immediately, garnished with orange slices.

**SERVES 8
as part of a tapas
meal**

2 garlic cloves,
finely chopped

1 Spanish onion,
finely chopped

2 tsp finely grated
lemon rind

2 tbsp lemon juice

1 tsp fresh thyme
leaves

1 tsp ground coriander

1 tsp ground cumin

2 tbsp red wine vinegar

125 ml/4 fl oz olive oil

1 kg/2 lb 4 oz lamb
fillet, cut into
2-cm/$^3/_4$-inch pieces

orange or lemon slices,
to garnish

MUSSELS WITH HERB & GARLIC BUTTER

SERVES 8
as part of a tapas
meal

800g/1 lb 12 oz fresh
mussels, in their shells

splash of dry white wine

1 bay leaf

85 g/3 oz butter

35 g/1¼ oz fresh
white or brown
breadcrumbs

4 tbsp chopped fresh
flat-leaf parsley, plus
extra sprigs to garnish

2 tbsp snipped fresh
chives

2 garlic cloves,
finely chopped

salt and pepper

lemon wedges,
to serve

Clean the mussels by scrubbing or scraping the shells and pulling out any beards that are attached to them. Discard any with broken shells and any that refuse to close when tapped. Put the mussels in a colander and rinse well under cold running water.

Put the mussels in a large saucepan and add a splash of wine and the bay leaf. Cook, covered, over a high heat for 5 minutes, shaking the saucepan occasionally, or until the mussels are opened. Drain the mussels and discard any that remain closed.

Shell the mussels, reserving one half of each shell. Arrange the mussels, in their half shells, in a large, shallow, ovenproof serving dish.

Melt the butter and pour into a small bowl.

Add the breadcrumbs, parsley, chives, garlic, and salt and pepper to taste, and mix well together. Leave until the butter has set slightly. Using your fingers or 2 teaspoons, take a large pinch of the herb and butter mixture and use to fill each mussel shell, pressing it down well. Chill the filled mussels in the refrigerator until ready to serve.

To serve, preheat the oven to 230°C/450°F/ Gas Mark 8. Bake the mussels in the oven for 10 minutes, or until hot. Serve immediately, garnished with parsley sprigs and accompanied by lemon wedges to squeeze over them.

CHORIZO & MUSHROOM KEBABS

Heat the olive oil in a frying pan over a medium heat. Add the chorizo and fry for 20 seconds, stirring.

Add the mushrooms and continue frying for a further 1–2 minutes until the mushrooms begin to brown and absorb the fat in the frying pan.

Thread a green pepper square, a piece of chorizo and a mushroom on to a wooden cocktail stick. Continue until all the ingredients are used. Serve hot or at room temperature with crusty bread.

MAKES 25

2 tbsp olive oil

25 pieces chorizo sausage, each about 1-cm/$\frac{1}{2}$-inch square (about 100 g/3$\frac{1}{2}$ oz)

25 button mushrooms, wiped and stalks removed

1 green pepper, grilled, peeled and cut into 25 squares

crusty bread, to serve

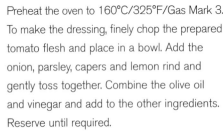 PRAWNS WRAPPED IN HAM

MAKES 16

16 raw tiger prawns

16 thin slices serrano
ham or Parma ham

extra-virgin Spanish
olive oil, for brushing

**TOMATO-CAPER
DRESSING**

2 tomatoes, peeled and
deseeded

1 small red onion, very
finely chopped

4 tbsp very finely
chopped fresh parsley

1 tbsp capers in brine,
drained, rinsed and
chopped

finely grated rind of
1 large lemon

4 tbsp extra-virgin
Spanish olive oil

1 tbsp sherry vinegar

Preheat the oven to 160°C/325°F/Gas Mark 3. To make the dressing, finely chop the prepared tomato flesh and place in a bowl. Add the onion, parsley, capers and lemon rind and gently toss together. Combine the olive oil and vinegar and add to the other ingredients. Reserve until required.

Pull the heads off the prawns and peel, leaving the tails intact. Cut along the length of the back of each prawn and remove and discard the dark vein. Rinse and pat dry. Wrap a slice of ham around each prawn and brush with a little oil. Place the prawns in a heatproof dish large enough to hold them in a single layer. Bake in the preheated oven for 10 minutes.

Transfer the prawns to a serving platter and spoon the dressing over or serve it in a bowl on the side. Serve immediately, or leave to cool to room temperature.

Spanish Sauces & Dips

FRESH SALMON IN MOJO SAUCE

**SERVES 8
as part of a tapas
meal**

4 fresh salmon fillets,
weighing about 750 g/
1 lb 10 oz in total

3 tbsp Spanish olive oil

1 fresh flat-leaf parsley
sprig, to garnish

salt and pepper

MOJO SAUCE

2 garlic cloves, peeled

2 tsp paprika

1 tsp ground cumin

5 tbsp Spanish
extra-virgin olive oil

2 tbsp white wine
vinegar

salt

To prepare the mojo sauce, put the garlic, paprika and cumin in the bowl of a food processor fitted with the metal blade and, using a pulsing action, blend for 1 minute to mix well together. With the motor still running, add 1 tablespoon of the olive oil, drop by drop, through the feeder tube. When it has been added, scrape down the sides of the bowl with a spatula, then very slowly continue to pour in the oil in a thin, steady stream, until all the oil has been added and the sauce has slightly thickened. Add the vinegar and blend for a further 1 minute. Season the sauce with salt to taste.

To prepare the salmon, remove the skin, cut each fillet in half widthways, then cut lengthways into 2-cm/³/₄-inch thick slices, discarding any bones. Season the pieces of fish to taste with salt and pepper.

Heat the olive oil in a large, heavy-based frying pan. When hot, add the pieces of fish and fry for about 10 minutes, depending on its thickness, turning occasionally until cooked and browned on both sides.

Transfer the salmon to a warmed serving dish, drizzle over some of the mojo sauce and serve hot, garnished with parsley and accompanied by the remaining sauce in a small serving bowl.

COURGETTE FRITTERS WITH PINE KERNEL SAUCE

To make the pine kernel sauce put the pine kernels and garlic in a food processor and blend to form a purée. With the motor still running, gradually add the olive oil, lemon juice and water to form a smooth sauce. Stir in the parsley and season to taste with salt and pepper. Turn into a serving bowl.

To prepare the courgettes, cut them diagonally into thin slices about 5 mm/¼ inch thick. Put the flour and paprika in a polythene bag and mix together. Beat the egg and milk together in a large bowl.

Add the courgette slices to the flour mixture and toss well together until coated. Shake off the excess flour. Heat the sunflower oil in a large, heavy-based frying pan to a depth of about 1 cm/½ inch. Dip the courgette slices, one at a time, into the egg mixture, then slip them into the hot oil. Fry the courgette slices, in batches of a single layer so that they do not overcrowd the frying pan, for 2 minutes, or until crisp and golden brown.

Using a slotted spoon, remove the courgette fritters from the pan and drain on kitchen paper. Continue until all the courgette slices have been fried.

Serve the courgette fritters piping hot, lightly sprinkled with sea salt. Accompany with the pine kernel sauce, garnished with dill.

SERVES 8
as part of a tapas meal

450 g/1 lb baby courgettes

3 tbsp plain flour

1 tsp paprika

1 large egg

2 tbsp milk

sunflower oil, for shallow-frying

coarse sea salt

PINE KERNEL SAUCE

100 g/3½ oz pine kernels

1 garlic clove, peeled

3 tbsp Spanish extra-virgin olive oil

1 tbsp lemon juice

3 tbsp water

1 tbsp chopped fresh flat-leaf parsley

salt and pepper

dill sprig, to garnish

NEW POTATOES WITH CHILLI SAUCE

Place the potatoes in a steamer set over a saucepan of boiling water. Cover and steam for 30 minutes, or until tender.

Meanwhile, make the sauce. Place the garlic, chillies and paprika in a mortar and grind to a paste with a pestle. Season to taste with salt, then gradually work in the vinegar. Finally, work in the olive oil.

Transfer the potatoes to warmed serving dishes and serve immediately with the chilli sauce.

Provide cocktail sticks for skewering and dipping the potatoes.

**SERVES 4–6
as part of a tapas
meal**

450 g/1 lb new
potatoes, unpeeled

2 garlic cloves, chopped

2 dried red chillies,
lightly crushed

1 tbsp paprika

2 tbsp sherry vinegar

150 ml/5 fl oz olive oil

salt

GREEN BEANS IN TOMATO SAUCE

Melt the butter in a large, heavy-based frying pan. Add the garlic and spring onions and cook over a medium heat, stirring occasionally, for 3–4 minutes. Add the beans and cook, stirring frequently, for a further 4 minutes.

Add the tomatoes with their can juices, pine kernels, lemon juice and bay leaf and season to taste with salt and pepper. Reduce the heat and leave to simmer gently for 30 minutes, or until the beans are tender and the sauce is pulpy.

Remove and discard the bay leaf. Taste and adjust the seasoning if necessary. Transfer to warmed serving dishes and serve hot.

**SERVES 6
as part of a tapas
meal**

25 g/1 oz butter

2 garlic cloves,
finely chopped

2 spring onions,
finely chopped

1 kg/2 lb 4 oz French
beans, cut into
2.5-cm/1-inch lengths

700 g/1 lb 9 oz canned
chopped tomatoes

1 tbsp pine kernels

1 tbsp lemon juice

1 bay leaf

salt and pepper

BATTERED PRAWNS & CORIANDER DIP

SERVES 4
as part of a tapas meal

12 raw prawns

1 egg

125 ml/4 fl oz water

115 g/4 oz plain flour

1 tsp cayenne pepper

vegetable oil, for deep-frying

orange wedges, to garnish

CORIANDER DIP

1 large bunch of fresh coriander, roughly chopped

3 garlic cloves, chopped

2 tbsp tomato purée

2 tbsp lemon juice

1 tbsp grated lemon rind

1¹/₂ tbsp sugar

1 tsp ground cumin

5 tbsp olive oil

First make the coriander dip. Place the coriander, garlic, tomato purée, lemon juice, lemon rind, sugar and cumin in a food processor or blender and process until combined. With the motor still running, gradually add the olive oil through the feeder tube until fully incorporated. Scrape into a bowl, cover with clingfilm and leave to chill until required.

Pull the heads off the prawns and peel, leaving the tails intact. Cut along the length of the back of each prawn and remove and discard the dark vein. Rinse under cold running water, then pat dry with kitchen paper.

Whisk the egg with the water in a small bowl. Gradually sift in the flour and cayenne, whisking constantly until smooth.

Heat the vegetable oil in a deep-fryer or large saucepan to 180–190°C/350–375°F, or until a cube of bread browns in 30 seconds. Holding the prawns by their tails, dip them into the batter, one at a time, shaking off any excess. Add the prawns to the oil and deep-fry for 2–3 minutes, or until crisp. Remove with a slotted spoon and drain well on kitchen paper. Serve immediately, garnished with orange wedges. Serve the coriander dip separately.

TINY SPANISH MEATBALLS IN ALMOND SAUCE

To prepare the meatballs, put the bread in a bowl, add the water and leave to soak for 5 minutes. With your hands, squeeze out the water and return the bread to the dried bowl. Add the pork, onion, garlic, parsley and egg, then season generously with grated nutmeg and a little salt and pepper. Knead the ingredients well together to form a smooth mixture.

Spread some flour on a plate. With floured hands, shape the meat mixture into about 30 equal-sized balls, then roll each meatball again in flour until coated.

Heat the olive oil in a large, heavy-based frying pan, add the meatballs, in batches so that they do not overcrowd the pan, and fry for 4–5 minutes, or until browned on all sides. Using a slotted spoon, remove the meatballs from the pan and set aside.

To make the almond sauce, heat the olive oil in the same frying pan in which the meatballs were fried. Break the bread into pieces, add to the pan with the almonds and fry gently, stirring frequently, until the bread and almonds are golden brown. Add the garlic and fry for a further 30 seconds, then pour in the wine and boil for 1–2 minutes. Season to taste with salt and pepper and allow to cool slightly.

Transfer the almond mixture to a food processor. Pour in the vegetable stock and blend the mixture until smooth. Return the sauce to the frying pan.

Carefully add the fried meatballs to the almond sauce and simmer for 25 minutes, or until the meatballs are tender. Taste the sauce and season with salt and pepper if necessary.

Transfer the cooked meatballs and almond sauce to a warmed serving dish, then add a squeeze of lemon juice to taste and sprinkle with chopped parsley to garnish. Serve piping hot, accompanied by chunks or slices of crusty bread for mopping up the almond sauce.

**SERVES 6–8
as part of a tapas
meal**

55 g/2 oz white or brown bread, crusts removed

3 tbsp water

450 g/1 lb fresh lean pork mince

1 large onion, finely chopped

1 garlic clove, crushed

2 tbsp chopped fresh flat-leaf parsley, plus extra to garnish

1 egg, beaten

freshly grated nutmeg

salt and pepper

flour, for coating

2 tbsp Spanish olive oil

squeeze of lemon juice

crusty bread, to serve

ALMOND SAUCE

2 tbsp Spanish olive oil

25 g/1 oz white or brown bread

115 g/4 oz blanched almonds

2 garlic cloves, finely chopped

150 ml/5 fl oz dry white wine

salt and pepper

425 ml/15 fl oz vegetable stock

AUBERGINE & PEPPER DIP

**SERVES 6–8
as part of a tapas
meal**

2 large aubergines

2 red peppers

4 tbsp Spanish olive oil

2 garlic cloves,
roughly chopped

grated rind and juice of
$1/2$ lemon

1 tbsp chopped fresh
coriander, plus extra
sprigs to garnish

$1/2$–1 tsp paprika

salt and pepper

bread or toast, to serve

Preheat the oven to 190°C/375°F/Gas Mark 5. Prick the skins of the aubergines and peppers all over with a fork and brush with 1 tablespoon of the olive oil. Put on a baking tray and bake in the oven for 45 minutes, or until the skins are beginning to turn black, the flesh of the aubergine is very soft and the peppers are deflated.

When the vegetables are cooked, put them in a bowl and immediately cover tightly with a clean, damp tea towel. Alternatively, you can put the vegetables in a polythene bag. Leave them for about 15 minutes until they are cool enough to handle.

When the vegetables have cooled, cut the aubergines in half lengthways, carefully scoop out the flesh and discard the skin. Cut the aubergine flesh into large chunks. Remove and discard the stem, core and seeds from the peppers and cut the flesh into large pieces.

Heat the remaining olive oil in a large, heavy-based frying pan, add the aubergine flesh and pepper pieces and fry for 5 minutes. Add the garlic and fry for a further 30 seconds.

Turn all the contents of the frying pan on to kitchen paper to drain, then transfer to the bowl of a food processor. Add the lemon rind and juice, the chopped coriander, the paprika, and salt and pepper according to taste, and blend until a speckled purée is formed.

Turn the aubergine and pepper dip into a serving bowl. Serve warm, at room temperature, or leave to cool for 30 minutes, then chill in the refrigerator for at least 1 hour and serve cold. Garnish with coriander sprigs and accompany with thick slices of bread or toast for dipping.

CHEESE PUFFS WITH FIERY TOMATO SALSA

To make the salsa, heat the olive oil in a saucepan, add the onion and fry for 5 minutes, or until softened but not browned. Add the garlic and fry for a further 30 seconds. Add the wine and allow to bubble, then add all the remaining salsa ingredients to the saucepan and simmer, uncovered, for 10–15 minutes, or until a thick sauce is formed. Spoon into a serving bowl and set aside until ready to serve.

Meanwhile, prepare the cheese puffs. Sift the flour onto a plate or sheet of greaseproof paper. Put the olive oil and water in a saucepan and slowly bring to the boil. As soon as the water boils, remove the saucepan from the heat and quickly tip in the flour all at once. Using a wooden spoon, beat the mixture well until it is smooth and leaves the sides of the saucepan.

Leave the mixture to cool for 1–2 minutes, then gradually add the eggs, beating hard after each addition and keeping the mixture stiff. Add the cheese and paprika, season to taste with salt and pepper and mix well together. You can store the mixture in the refrigerator at this stage until you are ready to fry the cheese puffs.

Just before serving the cheese puffs, heat the groundnut oil in a deep fryer to 180–190°C/350–375°F, or until a cube of bread browns in 30 seconds. Drop teaspoonfuls of the prepared mixture, in batches, into the hot oil and fry for 2–3 minutes, turning once, or until golden brown and crispy. They should rise to the surface of the oil and puff up. Drain well on kitchen paper.

Serve the puffs piping hot, accompanied by the fiery salsa for dipping and cocktail sticks to spear the puffs.

**SERVES 8
as part of a tapas meal**

70 g/2$\frac{1}{2}$ oz plain flour

50 ml/2 fl oz Spanish olive oil

150 ml/5 fl oz water

2 eggs, beaten

55 g/2 oz Manchego, Parmesan, Cheddar, Gouda or Gruyère cheese, finely grated

$\frac{1}{2}$ tsp paprika

salt and pepper

groundnut oil, for deep-frying

FIERY TOMATO SALSA

2 tbsp Spanish olive oil

1 small onion, finely chopped

1 garlic clove, crushed

splash of dry white wine

400 g/14 oz canned chopped tomatoes

1 tbsp tomato purée

$\frac{1}{4}$–$\frac{1}{2}$ tsp red chilli pepper flakes

dash of Tabasco sauce

pinch of sugar

salt and pepper

fresh flat-leaf parsley, to garnish

BABY POTATOES WITH AÏOLI

SERVES 6–8
as part of a tapas
meal

450 g/1 lb baby new
potatoes

1 tbsp chopped fresh
flat-leaf parsley

salt

AÏOLI

1 large egg yolk, at
room temperature

1 tbsp white wine
vinegar or lemon juice

2 large garlic cloves,
peeled

5 tbsp Spanish
extra-virgin olive oil

5 tbsp sunflower oil

salt and pepper

To make the aïoli, put the egg yolk, vinegar, garlic, and salt and pepper to taste, in the bowl of a food processor fitted with a metal blade and blend well together. With the motor still running, very slowly add the olive oil, then the sunflower oil, drop by drop at first, then, when it begins to thicken, in a slow, steady stream until the sauce is thick and smooth.

For this recipe, the aïoli should be a little thin so that it coats the potatoes. To ensure this, quickly blend in 1 tablespoon water so that it forms the consistency of sauce.

To prepare the potatoes, cut them in half or quarters to make bite-sized pieces. If they are very small, you can leave them whole. Put the potatoes in a large saucepan of cold, salted water and bring to the boil. Reduce the heat and simmer for 7 minutes, or until just tender. Drain well, then turn out into a large bowl.

While the potatoes are still warm, pour over the aïoli sauce and gently toss the potatoes in it. Adding the sauce to the potatoes while they are still warm will help them to absorb the garlic flavour. Leave for about 20 minutes to allow the potatoes to marinate in the sauce.

Transfer the potatoes with aïoli to a warmed serving dish, sprinkle over the parsley and salt to taste and serve warm. Alternatively, the dish can be prepared ahead and stored in the refrigerator, but return it to room temperature before serving.

STEAK BITES WITH CHILLI SAUCE

Heat half the olive oil in a heavy-based saucepan. Add the onion and cook over a low heat, stirring occasionally, for 5 minutes, or until softened. Add the paprika, garlic and chilli and cook for a further 2–3 minutes, then stir in the tomatoes with their juices, wine, tomato purée, vinegar and sugar. Simmer gently for 15–20 minutes, or until thickened.

Meanwhile, heat a heavy-based frying pan or griddle pan over a high heat and brush with the remaining olive oil. Season the steaks to taste with pepper and rub with the Tabasco sauce, then add to the pan. Cook for 1–1½ minutes on each side, or until browned. Reduce the heat and cook, turning once, for 3 minutes for rare, 4–5 minutes for medium or 5–7 minutes for well done. Remove from the heat and keep warm.

Transfer the sauce to a food processor or blender and process until fairly smooth. Transfer to a serving bowl, season to taste with salt and pepper and stir in the parsley.

Transfer the steaks to a chopping board and cut into bite-sized pieces. Spear with wooden cocktail sticks, place on serving plates and serve immediately with the sauce.

**SERVES 4–6
as part of a tapas
meal**

2 tbsp olive oil

1 onion, chopped

1 tsp paprika

1 garlic clove,
finely chopped

1 fresh red chilli,
deseeded and sliced

400 g/14 oz canned
chopped tomatoes

2 tbsp dry white wine

1 tbsp tomato purée

1 tbsp sherry vinegar

2 tsp sugar

2 rump steaks, about
175–225 g/6–8 oz each

2 tsp Tabasco sauce

1 tbsp chopped fresh
parsley

salt and pepper

CHICKEN LIVERS IN SHERRY SAUCE

**SERVES 6
as part of a tapas
meal**

450 g/1 lb chicken
livers

2 tbsp Spanish olive oil

1 small onion,
finely chopped

2 garlic cloves,
finely chopped

100 ml/3^1/$_2$ fl oz dry
Spanish sherry

2 tbsp chopped fresh
flat-leaf parsley

salt and pepper

crusty bread or toast,
to serve

If necessary, trim the chicken livers, cutting away any ducts and gristle, then cut them into small, bite-sized pieces.

Heat the olive oil in a large, heavy-based frying pan. Add the onion and fry for 5 minutes, or until softened but not browned. Add the garlic and fry for a further 30 seconds.

Add the chicken livers to the pan and fry for 2–3 minutes, stirring all the time, until they are firm and have changed colour on the outside but are still pink and soft in the centre. Using a slotted spoon, lift the chicken livers from the pan, transfer them to a large, warmed serving dish or several smaller ones and keep warm.

Add the sherry to the pan, increase the heat and let it bubble for 3–4 minutes to evaporate the alcohol and reduce slightly. At the same time, deglaze the pan by scraping and stirring all the bits on the base of the pan into the sauce with a wooden spoon. Season the sauce to taste with salt and pepper.

Pour the sherry sauce over the chicken livers and sprinkle over the parsley. Serve piping hot, accompanied by chunks or slices of crusty bread or toast to mop up the sherry sauce.

POTATO WEDGES WITH ROASTED GARLIC DIP

First, make the roasted garlic dip. Preheat the oven to 200°C/400°F/Gas Mark 6. Place the garlic cloves in an ovenproof dish, pour in the olive oil and toss to coat. Spread out in a single layer and roast in the preheated oven for 25 minutes, or until tender. Remove from the oven and leave until cool enough to handle.

Peel the garlic cloves, then place on a heavy chopping board and sprinkle with a little salt. Mash well with a fork until smooth. Scrape into a bowl and stir in the crème fraîche and mayonnaise. Season to taste with salt and paprika. Cover the bowl with clingfilm and leave to chill until ready to serve.

To cook the potatoes, cut each potato half into 3 wedges and place in a large bowl. Add the olive oil, garlic and salt and toss well. Transfer the wedges to a roasting tin, arrange in a single layer and roast in the preheated oven for 1–1¼ hours, or until crisp and golden.

Remove from the oven and transfer to serving bowls. Serve immediately, with the roasted garlic dip.

**SERVES 8
as part of a tapas meal**

1.3 kg/3 lb potatoes, unpeeled and halved

2 tbsp olive oil

1 garlic clove, finely chopped

2 tsp salt

ROASTED GARLIC DIP

2 garlic bulbs, separated into cloves

1 tbsp Spanish olive oil

5 tbsp crème fraîche or Greek-style yogurt

4 tbsp mayonnaise

paprika, to taste

salt

SARDINES WITH ROMESCO SAUCE

**SERVES 6
as part of a tapas
meal**

24 fresh sardines,
scaled, cleaned and
heads removed

115 g/4 oz plain flour

4 eggs, lightly beaten

250 g/9 oz fresh white
breadcrumbs

6 tbsp chopped fresh
parsley

4 tbsp chopped fresh
marjoram

vegetable oil,
for deep-frying

ROMESCO SAUCE

1 red pepper, halved
and deseeded

2 tomatoes, halved

4 garlic cloves

125 ml/4 fl oz olive oil

1 slice white bread,
diced

4 tbsp blanched
almonds

1 fresh red chilli,
deseeded and chopped

2 shallots, chopped

1 tsp paprika

2 tbsp red wine vinegar

2 tsp sugar

1 tbsp water

First make the sauce. Preheat the oven to 220°C/425°F/Gas Mark 7. Place the pepper, tomatoes and garlic in an ovenproof dish and drizzle over 1 tablespoon of the olive oil, turning to coat. Bake in the preheated oven for 20–25 minutes, then remove from the oven and cool. Peel off the skins and place the flesh in a food processor.

Heat 1 tablespoon of the remaining oil in a frying pan. Add the bread and almonds and cook over a low heat for a few minutes, or until browned. Remove and drain on kitchen paper. Add the chilli, shallots and paprika to the pan and cook for a further 5 minutes, or until the shallots are softened.

Transfer the almond mixture and shallot mixture to the food processor and add the vinegar, sugar and water. Process to a paste. With the motor still running, gradually add the remaining oil through the feeder tube. Transfer to a bowl, cover and reserve.

Place the sardines, skin-side up, on a chopping board and press along the length of the spines with your thumbs. Turn over and remove and discard the bones. Place the flour and eggs in separate bowls. Mix the breadcrumbs and herbs together in a third bowl. Coat the fish in the flour, the eggs, then in the breadcrumbs.

Heat the vegetable oil in a large saucepan to 180–190°C/350–375°F, or until a cube of bread browns in 30 seconds. Deep-fry the fish for 4–5 minutes, or until golden and tender. Drain and serve with the sauce.

MOORISH BROAD BEAN DIP

If using fresh broad beans, bring a large saucepan of lightly salted water to the boil. Add the beans, then reduce the heat, cover and simmer for 7 minutes. Drain well, refresh under cold running water and drain again. Remove and discard the outer skins. If using frozen beans, leave to thaw completely, then remove and discard the outer skins.

Heat one tablespoon of the olive oil in a frying pan. Add the garlic, onion and cumin and cook over a low heat, stirring occasionally, until the onion is softened and translucent.

Add the broad beans and cook, stirring frequently, for 5 minutes.

Remove the frying pan from the heat and transfer the mixture to a food processor or blender. Add the lemon juice, the remaining olive oil, water and mint and process to a purée. Season to taste with salt and pepper.

Scrape the purée back into the frying pan and heat gently until warm. Transfer to individual serving bowls, dust lightly with paprika and serve with dippers of your choice.

**SERVES 6
as part of a tapas
meal**

500 g/1 lb 2 oz shelled
fresh or frozen broad
beans

5 tbsp olive oil

1 garlic clove,
finely chopped

1 onion, finely chopped

1 tsp ground cumin

1 tbsp lemon juice

175 ml/6 fl oz water

1 tbsp chopped fresh
mint

salt and pepper

paprika, to garnish

raw vegetables, crusty
bread, or breadsticks,
to serve

index